Toward a More Visual Literacy

Toward a More Visual Literacy

Shifting the Paradigm with Digital Tools and Young Adult Literature

Edited by Jennifer S. Dail, Shelbie Witte, and Steven T. Bickmore

ROWMAN & LITTLEFIELD
Lanham • Boulder • New York • London

Published by Rowman & Littlefield
A wholly owned subsidiary of the Rowman & Littlefield Publishing Group, Inc.
4501 Forbes Boulevard, Suite 200, Lanham, Maryland 20706
www.rowman.com

Unit A, Whitacre Mews, 26–34 Stannary Street, London SE11 4AB

Copyright © 2018 by Jennifer S. Dail, Shelbie Witte, and Steven T. Bickmore

All rights reserved. No part of this book may be reproduced in any form or by any electronic or mechanical means, including information storage and retrieval systems, without written permission from the publisher, except by a reviewer who may quote passages in a review.

British Library Cataloguing in Publication Information Available

Library of Congress Cataloging-in-Publication Data Is Available
ISBN 978-1-4758-3566-3 (cloth: alk. paper)
ISBN 978-1-4758-3567-0 (pbk: alk. paper)
ISBN 978-1-4758-3568-7 (electronic)

∞™ The paper used in this publication meets the minimum requirements of American National Standard for Information Sciences—Permanence of Paper for Printed Library Materials, ANSI/NISO Z39.48–1992.

Printed in the United States of America

Contents

Foreword   vii
Lisa Scherff

Acknowledgments   ix

Introduction: Positioning Students as Creators in the Classroom   1
Jennifer S. Dail and Shelbie Witte

PART I: CLASSROOM CONTEXTS: HELPING STUDENTS VISUALIZE DIGITALLY   7

1. "It's about More Than Words": Reading *All American Boys* in a Social Digital Reading Environment   9
Sara B. Kajder

2. Flipping the Teaching of Young Adult Literature with Preservice Teachers   19
Amy Piotrowski

3. Socratic Learning Conversations: Ancient Practice Meets New Technology   27
Jenny Cameron Paulsen and Matt Copeland

PART II: SOCIAL ENGAGEMENT: CONNECTING YOUTH BEYOND SCHOOL   39

4. Responding to Young Adult Literature through Civic Engagement   41
Kristen Hawley Turner and Dawn Reed

5	Social Media, Gaming, and Jay Gatsby: Integrating Youth Motifs with Youth Literacies in High School English *Alison Heron-Hruby, Lindsay Ellis Johnson, Dakoda Trenary, and Dallas Cox*	53
6	Infusing Young Adult Literature into the Virtual Classroom *Brooke Eisenbach, Paula Greathouse, and Jennifer Farnham*	63

PART III: CRITICAL INQUIRY: DIGGING DEEPER WITH YOUNG ADULT LITERATURE — 77

7	Emerging Media, Evolving Engagement: Expanding Teachers' Repertoires of Young Adult Literary Study and Response *Anna Smith and Robyn Seglem*	79
8	Seeing the World Differently: Remixing Young Adult Literature through Critical Lenses *Jennifer S. Dail and Aneté Vásquez*	91
9	"Song of Myself": A Digital Unit of Study Remixed *Fawn Canady, Kymberly Martin, and Chyllis E. Scott*	101

Appendix A	119
Appendix B	123
Index	125
About the Editors	131
About the Contributors	133

Foreword

I was honored to be asked to write the foreword to this book. As a classroom teacher, I struggle daily between/among a range of tensions pushing and pulling me: providing my students with authentic texts to read, discuss, and respond to; preparing my students for mandated high-stakes tests; incorporating technology in meaningful and interesting ways; and, making my classroom a safe space where students feel free to express themselves. Reading this edited collection provided me with a range of responses and ideas to incorporate immediately.

It is no accident that all three parts of this volume—"Classroom Contexts: Helping Students Visualize Digitally," Social Engagement: Connecting Youth beyond School, and "Critical Enquiry: Digging Deeper with Young Adult Literature"—emphasize action with and among students and texts. We cannot just put resources (texts, technology, tools) into classrooms; we must *help* students interact with them; we must *connect* them to students' lives outside of school; and we must help students learn to *dig deeply* with them. Such work is not just a matter of engagement but an issue of providing students with the human experience. "In an era when educational assessments are increasingly narrow, we need 'multiple channels of communication' beyond print to express human ways of knowing" (Freire, 1993, as cited in Miller and Bruce, 2017, 14).

This edited collection highlights ways that teachers can use a range of digital technologies to engage students meaningfully in reading, writing, and composing with and about young adult literature. And, books such as this are needed desperately in schools. When I first started teaching twenty years ago, nearly all my colleagues entered the profession after graduating from teacher education programs; however, now most my colleagues have no teacher training background at all. And I suspect this is the case in many places around the country. Without training in pedagogically sound ways to use traditional print texts and technology in their classrooms, it means that teachers are not providing their students with opportunities to learn literacy practices needed to navigate the twenty-first century. Books like this must get into their hands. I commend the editors for putting this volume together. They have offered readers a group of teachers and scholars who do not just offer "ideas" but put into practice tangible teaching practices in an understandable and straightforward way.

Reading the chapters I was struck by the multiple avenues that the authors considered to engage and teach: flipping instruction, remixing texts, integrating gaming, and so on are not just gimmicks (like so much of the technology sold to schools) to get students to pay attention but also ways to make students members of numerous discourse communities in thoughtful and sustainable ways. This participation and membership is a right that all students deserve. As Miller and Bruce (2017) contend, "It is a matter of social justice to allow students opportunities to use familiar and/or emergent technologies in mediated and meaningful educational inquiry. Not to do so limits the ability of their available expression, fosters a top-down approach to learning, and perpetuates a narrowed representation of student assessment" (18).

Lisa Scherff

REFERENCE

Miller, S., and D. Bruce. 2017. "Welcome to the 21st Century: New Literacies Stances to Support Student Learning with Digital Composing." *English Journal* 106 (3): 14–18.

Acknowledgments

More thanks than words can express to my husband Garth for always saying "go for it" when I dive into a project. To all of my students who introduce me to fresh perspectives and invite me into their classrooms, pushing me to do better each semester, thank you.

—Jennifer S. Dail

Heartfelt gratitude to Mike for supporting me, to KT and Tayler for inspiring me, and to all of my students for teaching *me* something every day.

—Shelbie Witte

I would like to thank my wife Dana for her support when I have my nose in a book. I would also like to thank all of my students over the years for their constant inspiration. Finally, a big thank you to colleagues, including classroom teachers and librarians who keep offering one more book to the kids they work with.

—Steven T. Bickmore

Introduction

Positioning Students as Creators in the Classroom

Jennifer S. Dail and Shelbie Witte

Credit line: istock.com/fstop123

Much has been written about the importance of considering technology and multimodal texts as part of the literacies we teach in twenty-first-century schools (Janks, 2012, 2014; Jenkins, 2013; Jenkins, Purushotma, Weigel, Clinton, and Robinson, 2009; Kress, 1999). Typically schools privilege written texts: however, considering multiple modes of literacy requires that teachers shift their focus toward genres of text that do not rely solely on linear, print texts.

The shift in focus needs to be not just on student consumption of these texts but also on student production of them. Such genres include visual texts. Kress (1999) points out that as visual language becomes more predominant in public modes of communication, "written language is being displaced from its hitherto unchallenged central position in the semiotic landscape, and that the visual is taking over many of the functions of written language" (68). This shift to the visual requires that teachers consider how students read images in the classroom, address visual literacy, and use images to construct critical literacy.

ADOLESCENTS' LITERACY PRACTICES

In a commentary on theorizing adolescents' literacies for classroom practice, Alvermann (2008) acknowledges that we might look at the out-of-school literacy practices of students and shrug them off as what the kids do and continue not to sanction them within the space of school. Yet she points out that these "literacies [are] so powerfully motivating that young people are more and more willing to invest a substantial amount of time and effort in creating content to share with others online" (9). Why would we not want to leverage this in our classrooms? This book demonstrates practical ways in which teachers are accomplishing integrating students' online literacies their classrooms.

Alvermann also notes that "young people are often fans of content thought to be inappropriate (or irrelevant at best) to most school curricula" (10). This applies to not only digital content and the ways students tinker with it to create new content but texts as well. Every teacher knows that if you tell a student a book is inappropriate for some reason, it is the book they are more likely to seek out. Jennifer's own experience taught her that in the sixth grade when other girls were passing around copies of Judy Blume's *Forever*. The teacher took the books away and told us that we shouldn't be reading them.

As most adolescents are, we were resourceful and found copies at the public library to check out. It only motivated us more to read the book, and it was definitely more interesting than anything in the prescribed reading anthology with its contrived excerpts and questions to answer after reading them. That is precisely why young adult (YA) literature is so appealing to students. It is real and gritty, which is why few YA novels are sanctioned in school curricula. At best, they are allowed as independent or supplemental reading.

STANDARDS: THE BASIS FOR CLASSROOM PRACTICE

The International Society for Technology in Education (ISTE) articulates standards that "are designed to empower student voice and ensure that learning is a student-driven process of exploration, creativity and discovery no matter where they or their teachers are in the thoughtful integration of ed tech" (2017). Four of these seven standards fit into the work presented in this book: empowered learner, knowledge constructor, innovative designer, and creative communicator.

Two of the remaining four are implied within many of the chapters within this book: digital citizen and global collaborator. When students are empowered learners, they "leverage technology to take an active role in choosing, achieving and demonstrating competency in their learning goals" (ISTE, Standard 1). This empowerment shifts the dynamics in the classroom to give students more ownership of their learning and to have the teacher positioned as facilitator of that learning environment. When students are empowered, they become the knowledge constructors, innovative designers, and creative communicators articulated in the standards. As knowledge constructors, "students critically curate a variety of resources using digital tools to construct knowledge, produce creative artifacts and make meaningful learning experiences for themselves and others" (ISTE, Standard 3).

As part of constructing knowledge, students should move into designing a variety of products to share that knowledge. In doing so, "Students use a variety of technologies within a design process to identify and solve problems by creating new, useful or imaginative solutions" (ISTE, Standard 4). This variety of technologies results in multimodal products where students draw from an array of modes to creatively communicate their message. As creative communicators, "Express themselves creatively for a variety of purposes using the platforms, tools, styles, formats and digital media appropriate to their goals" (ISTE, Standard 6).

This sort of digital work that positions students as producers of content in their learning process requires that they understand a variety of rhetorical contexts, tools, and audiences to successfully accomplish their goals.

PEDAGOGICAL CONSIDERATIONS

In considering the role of visual and multimodal texts in the classroom, teachers have to examine *how* they are asking students to interact with these texts. Are we positioning students as consumers of the media they study, or are we inviting them to enter and contribute to the conversation through the production of their own texts? As we move toward more visual literacy and modes of authorship (e.g., blogs, wikis, podcasts, and video production) allowed by Web 2.0 (Rozema), production becomes increasingly important to students' critical consumption of multimedia texts.

Our students already live and communicate in a virtual world connected by expansive networks. Selfe and Hawisher (2004) assert, "If literacy educators continue to define literacy in terms of alphabetic practices only, in ways that ignore, exclude, or devalue new media texts, they not only abdicate a professional responsibility to describe the ways in which humans are now communicating and making meaning, but they also run the risk of their curriculum no longer holding relevance for students who are" living and communicating in these digital environments (233). Part of the popularity of the web is its addition of graphic and verbal content to print media (Bolter, 2009). Multimodal literacy practices offer new modes to engage students in responding critically to literature, and to YA literature in particular.

YA literature is written for a target audience of twelve- to eighteen-year-olds—for adolescents. These are the books adolescents choose to read as opposed to those they are required to read for school. Beyond the parameters of school, adolescents also actively consume various media via technology and many even dabble in producing it. Therefore, it makes sense to examine ways texts written for adolescents can be combined with the digital tools they choose to use to craft more critical conversation around literary response and digital media consumption and production.

Technology offers us a "paradigm shift about how the students interact with the text and about the authority they take when responding to text and how we as teachers conceptualize ownership to invite students to use their own creativity as a tool for reading and for writing/producing. Technology simply offer[s] a medium through which we might accomplish that" (Dail and Thompson, 2016, 3). That paradigm shift often embodies participatory cultures in our classrooms, or at least starts to move classroom practices in that direction (Kupiainen, 2013).

Supporting students in responding to literature is one means of empowering them with interpretive authority as readers and creating a classroom culture where student contributions matter. Bringing literary response into practice with characteristics of participatory culture expands on the student-centered, critical aspects of both.

This book explores adolescents' authentic uses of digital media in response to YA literature. Adolescents take up technology in ways many of us who did not grow up with technology cannot imagine, and often students are more proficient with digital technologies than we—their teachers—are. They appropriate technology to mediate social identities, enter cultural conversations, interact with others, and construct out-of-school literacy practices with authentic meaning to them. Sometimes teachers are reluctant to integrate larger technology projects in the curriculum because they recognize this gape and because we don't want to look like we know less than our students.

Yet, Selfe (1999) argues that it is teachers' "lack of familiarity with technology . . . that can provide the intellectual perspective we need to begin making changes. By *paying attention* to the unfamiliar subject of technology . . . we may learn some important lessons about how to go about making change in literacy instruction" (134). We believe this *paying attention* to technology is necessary in helping our students develop twenty-first-century literacies where they do more than consume technology but critically think about and engage with it to enter the conversations around YA literature as producers. This book explores ways adolescents read and engage with the world around them to construct meaning and to examine how teachers can implement these practices within their own classrooms.

Organization of the Book

This book is organized into three parts addressing a scaffolded approach to the integration of digital media production as part of literary responses to YA novels. The first part, "Classroom Contexts: Helping Students Visualize Digitally," focuses on using digital tools to facilitate student response to literature within the classroom. In this part, students are positioned primarily as knowledge constructors (ISTE, 2017) as they begin to use technology to create knowledge from literature study.

The second part, "Social Engagement: Connecting Youth beyond School," focuses on creating a participatory culture where students are trying to consciously connect with others beyond the physical walls of the classroom to extend the discourse into a virtual space. In this part, students are positioned as innovative designers as they begin to create products that present a new perspective on literature (ISTE, 2017).

The third part, "Critical Inquiry: Digging Deeper with Young Adult Literature," focuses on using the technology to support students in making broader and deeper connections with the texts. In this part, students are also positioned as innovative designers as they use a variety of critical stances to create more detailed products grounded in more complex networks of classroom discourse (ISTE, 2017). Throughout the chapters in this book, students are positioned as creative communicators who are using technology in a variety of ways to express their learning and understanding of texts (ISTE, 2017).

The contributors to this book are real classroom teachers and teacher educators committed to taking up digital work in their classrooms as a means to support students in more authentic engagement with literature. While the approaches presented will work with any literature you bring into your classroom, regardless of whether or not it is YA literature, we think they work particularly well with it because of the intersections created among students' literacy interests and practices.

Our goal was to create a book that offers practical classroom examples, and we hope that these examples allow teachers to enter into this sort of work regardless of their experience level with it. We hope that these examples encourage teachers to take the risk of tinkering and geeking out with their students, as we believe that builds a stronger classroom community and a more engaged literate youth.

REFERENCES

Alvermann, D. 2008. "Commentary: Why Bother Theorizing Adolescents' Online Literacies for Classroom Practice and Research?" *Journal for Adolescent & Adult Literacy* 52 (1): 8–19. doi:10.1698/JAAL.52.1.2.

Bolter, J. D. 2009. "Hypertext and the Question of Visual Literacy." In *Handbook of Literacy and Technology: Transformations in a Post-typographic World*, edited by D. Reinkin, M. C. McKenna, L. D. Labbo, and R. D. Kieffer, 3–15. Mahwah, NJ: Lawrence Erlbaum Associates.

Dail, J. 2011. "Digital Storytelling: The Story of Students' Literary Responses and Pedagogical Approaches." In *Teachers as Avatars: English Studies in the Digital Age*, edited by L. R. Davis and L. Stewart, 179–92. New York: Hampton Press.

Dail, J. S., and N. Thompson. 2016. "Talking Back: Remix as a Tool to Help Students Exercise Authority When Making Meaning." *ALAN Review* 43 (3): 35–48.

International Society for Technology in Education. 2017. *ISTE Standards for Students*. https://www.iste.org/standards/standards/for-students.

Jenkins, H., and W. Kelley. 2013. *Reading in a Participatory Culture: Remixing Moby Dick in the English Classroom*. New York: Teachers College Press.

Jenkins, H., R. Purushotma, M. Weigel, K. Clinton, and A. J. Robinson. 2009. *Confronting the Challenges of Participatory Culture: Media Education for the 21st Century*. Cambridge, MA: MIT Press.

Kress, G. 1999. "English at the Crossroads: Rethinking Curricula of Communication in the Context of the Turn to the Visual." In *Passions, Pedagogies, and 21st Century Technologies*, edited by C. L. Selfe and G. E. Hawisher, 66–88. Urbana, IL: National Council of Teachers of English.

Kupiainen, R. 2013. *Media and Digital Literacies in Secondary School*. New York: Peter Lang Publishing, Inc.

Rozema, R. 2007. "The Book Report, Version 2.0: Podcasting on Young Adult Novels." *English Journal* 97 (1): 31–36.

Selfe, C. L. 1999. *Technology and Literacy in the Twenty-First Century: The Importance of Paying Attention*. Carbondale, IL: Southern Illinois University Press.

Selfe, C. L., and G. E. Hawisher. 2004. *Literate Lives in the Information Age*. New York: Routledge.

Part I

CLASSROOM CONTEXTS
Helping Students Visualize Digitally

Chapter 1

"It's about More Than Words": Reading *All American Boys* in a Social Digital Reading Environment

Sara B. Kajder

This chapter explores a social digital reading project pairs two classes of eighth graders in southeastern Georgia and in southwestern Pennsylvania. Their demographics are similar—highly diverse student populations from high-poverty communities, low reading performance on standardized tests, and both offering 1:1 programs outfitting students with continuous access to a Wi-Fi-connected laptop or Chromebook. The project, to collaboratively and socially read *All American Boys* by Jason Reynolds and Brendan Kiely, was designed to reveal, uncover, and engage with what made students' contexts, experiences, and perspectives both distinct *and* unified.

Using a collaborative and multimodal digital reading platform, Glose.com, both classes read the text online using written text, images, and video to annotate. The students and their teachers needed to develop new skills as social digital readers. At the onset, only ten of the forty-eight students involved in the project identified themselves as readers outside of assigned reading. All but four students had recently tested as reading at least two years beneath grade level using district reading assessments. Where both teachers had highly curated classroom libraries featuring recent young adult (YA) titles, this was the first whole class YA studied in either context.

In both classrooms, students were skilled at using digital devices to share content through Google Classroom or to exercise skills within prepackaged comprehension and fluency programs. They did not have experience using digital tools to create, annotate, or simply read. Similarly, neither classroom teacher had read a digital book prior to this project. Despite that, both teachers shared the goal to use technology to provide students with access to a text authentically relevant within the context of a task that would help build stronger readers.

WHY DIGITAL READING?

Through 1:1 programs, all students had access to wireless-connected devices and most carried individual smartphones. And yet, because of their low performance on standardized reading assessments, they were placed in English classrooms where reading digitally meant accessing text on a screen and keying in responses to multiple-choice comprehension questions. For this project, digital reading became more layered, multimodal, nuanced, and social.

Instead of thinking about digital reading as an outcome of the device or tool used to access text (Bauerlein, 2011), this project considers the *mindful* use of the tools to support a connective, social, multimodal, and engaged reading experience (Kajder, 2010; Kajder, Turner, and Hicks, 2016). Instead of thinking of new practices as replacing those that came before, this work is steeped in the thinking that emerging digital tools make possible new kinds of practices and change how we engage in the former ones. This is the work that is about "and" rather than "or."

Digital reading is also social, given that the online reading space allows for readers to interact with one another in and around the text through image, color, print text, and video. As literacy education has shifted from thinking about literacy to literacies, we have come to understand reading as nonlinear, multimodal, social, and collaborative (Kress, 2003). Further, in a shared, collaborative digital reading environment (e.g., Glose), the text itself becomes a participatory space, offering low barriers for participation and reflecting the idea that not everyone needs to participate in all aspects of the exchange but that the opportunity is present to all when they are ready (Jenkins, Purushotma, Weigel, Clinton, and Robison, 2009).

Physical access to digital tools does not mean that students know how to use those same tools to read, write, or learn. This secondary digital divide (Leu, Forzani, and Kennedy, 2015) was most evident in these two classrooms as low-performing readers were given increasingly reductive digital tasks focused on test preparation and less opportunities for collaborative, creative, and critical/evaluative work.

All but one student in the project reported having a networked smartphone that was indispensable in their out-of-school lives. However, those mobile literacy skills were quite different from those required in cultivating an intentional digital identity as a reader or in navigating a complex online environment for academic purposes (Kajder, 2010). An additional rationale for this project was for students to develop skills related to generating and composing digital content, collaborating with a virtual peer and audience, and curating and cultivating an academic digital footprint, given the paucity of similar experiences within their academic or out-of-school digital literacy learning.

UNPACKING THE PROJECT

This social digital reading project spanned five weeks, where students read in and outside of class and completed other curricular tasks. It was a collaboration between Ms. Hill in Georgia and Mr. Teel in Pennsylvania. Both graduated from the same teacher education program and had previously connected students on smaller-scale e-mail or Goodreads projects. As this was their first try at a large-scale collaborative, connected project, both chose to pilot this project with a single class, which shared thirty minutes of commonly scheduled time allowing for periodic connections via Google Hangouts.

Setting Up the Connection: Classroom Use of Glose

The teachers chose glose.com as the digital reading environment, given its ease of use, multimodal commenting/annotation capacities, and that it was available through both school systems' restrictive Internet filters. Reading in Glose meant logging in, accessing the desired text (with one copy purchased for each participating student through the Glose bookstore), and scrolling or paginating through a digital offering of the book. Where one could simply read using Glose, the added functionality related to annotation is what made for a social and multimodal reading experience.

At the time of this project, Glose readers could annotate through highlights, the addition of print notes, the use of images, or embedding video. Further, Glose allowed teachers to establish private reading groups specifically for their students, monitor student posts/comments across all groups on a single page, and comment and work within each reading groups' set of annotations.

Prior to beginning the project with students, teachers asked students to set up an account using their school e-mail. Then, teachers set up reading groups inside of Glose, merging their class lists to make groups of four to five readers who represented a mix of students from both schools. The functionality of Glose allowed each student to make private annotations or to share those annotations within the wider public of their reading group. Readers could also respond to the annotations of their peers through the same range of modalities.

It was important to Mr. Teel and Ms. Hill to not require a number or specific modality of the annotations that each student was expected to enter. Instead, they used a holistic scale (capturing the overall engagement across a three-day period of reading and responding on a four-point scale) and students' weekly reflections on their progress, contributions, and goals. They wanted participation to be genuine rather than reflective of a requirement, and they wanted to encourage self-regulation and responsibility among readers.

Establishing the Collaboration: Choosing All American Boys

Both teachers wanted to engage students in reading a YA novel and wanted them to make the selection. Both saw the necessity of choosing a text that was high interest and yet complex enough to evoke unpacking through the collective annotation that Glose supported. The initial list presented to their students included a range of award-winning titles, which were book talked or presented through a publisher's book trailer.

Initially, neither class was very excited about any of the titles—*Hunger Games*, *Unwound*, *Reality Boy*, and *The Giver*. As Ms. Hill explained, "There was something about the list that they saw as school rather than as something they *wanted* to read." She planned to speak with Mr. Teel that afternoon, not yet knowing his class had reacted similarly.

After that day's class, Antonio (PA) followed a trail of book trailers on YouTube between classes and found an interview with Jason Reynolds speaking about diversity. He was hooked. As Mr. Teel described, "He must have played that clip five times, staying past the bell and talking with kids about race and diversity and empathy. . . . I knew we needed to jump in with it as this was as animated as I had ever seen them be about an author." After finding a copy of *All American Boys*, Antonio came to Mr. Teel, offering, "I don't read. I *really* don't read. But this book is something else. It's messing with me. Get this one." With his help, Antonio wrote and shared a quick book talk with both classes, connecting Georgia through Google Hangouts.

The teachers asked students to capture their "vote" in an exit ticket. Not only was the vote unanimously in favor of the book, but the students' comments spoke to the appeal, offering that it "sounded real," "shaked me up already," "is about GA and PA," and "might give us a chance to legit talk." As Ms. Hill shared, "To get two different groups of kids in two different states to completely agree on a single book . . . we never saw that coming. But, in hindsight, we both knew the book and should have gotten there ourselves. There probably isn't a book that could better speak to our now than this one. It's hard but that is also in our favor."

Crafting Identities as Readers within Glose

This project involved two groups of students with the habits and identities of nonreaders, struggling readers, reluctant readers, dormant readers, and so forth. This unit challenged them to come into a text that presented real, immediate, raw context and content from the first chapter. Through the project, students reset or unlearned those identities. The teachers relied on the high appeal of *All American Boys* and the hook of the task, reading within a digital space that included peers who were 625 miles away. The task itself also disrupted what it meant to use technology in school, as students were invited to create, respond, and lever the tool to express their thinking—not to complete a checklist of tasks or key in A, B, or C.

"So Much More Than a Photo": Crafting an Avatar

One of the most significant aspects of helping students find success came before they opened the book. When establishing an account, students were directed to use their first names and last initial, in compliance with school policies. However, each student was invited to use a photo as an avatar, guided by his or her teachers to use his or her photo "as a reader." Taysha (GA) explained, "We started to take pictures behind books or in being nerdy readers. I added glasses. Jay made this huge stack of books and sort of peeked out from behind. It was a bit of a gas."

Both teachers underjudged the importance of these photos. Mr. Teel explained, "What I saw as play and silly wasn't at all that way. These photos were the introduction to their new group-mates in another state, almost as if they set the expectations that they *were* readers, contrary to every message school might have sent. They *were* readers here."

For some students, the avatar was an identity marker. Geo (PA) offered, "Hey, nobody in Georgia knew I wasn't a reader before. If I tried to do the thing with this book and with them, to them, I am a reader." A significant number of students in both classes used the image as a projected identity, and, as such, evolved their images as they read. Angel (GA) talked about her progression.

> First it was the book cover because I didn't know what to do. I don't read so how do I show up in a pic that way? Then, I met my group and we started into it cause the book is real stuff, police brutality, race.... I changed my pic so I was in it. First I drew a halo over the book (like my name) but by halfway, I made it a pic of me next to the book. Like a statement. I'm black. This book is about me. And, I'm a reader cause I don't just see words on the page. I see us all.

In their exit surveys at the close of the unit, all but two students identified the photo avatar as the second most important part of the project, behind the book itself.

"I Marked for Myself": Annotating to Discuss

Each class used *Notice and Note* (2012) strategies to teach annotation in previous units, so initial shared annotations were marginal tags noting which signposts they identified. The volatility of the first chapter added to these responses. Asha (GA) explained, "You get hit with hard stuff about race immediately and school don't talk about that. So, we shared what school thinks." In personal annotations, those not shared, students were posting questions, animated gifs, and initial video responses. As Jesse (PA) shared, "I was thinking on the page but I marked for myself. Now I see it as warming up for the group but then it was just me in my head."

When prompted by their teachers to also start using annotations to talk within the groups, students wrestled with the idea of questions. Jayson (PA) offered, "You ask questions when you don't understand. I understood too much. Plus, I wanted to be a reader so bad that I didn't want to ask something that might give up that it was hard." The turning point came after a mini-lesson where the teachers offered a think aloud that revealed their own struggles and questions as readers. Kesha (GA) described this as "them showing us that even really good readers ask a lot and that is what real reading makes you do."

As much as these students had to learn that questioning a text was not a sign of lack of skill or understanding, they also had to learn that their discussions were safe. Bo (PA) explained, "These are the things we don't even talk to our friends about—what we see and what we know. [The authors] made us do it. So, here we are doing the thing we don't do with a book that tells us we need to talk to make anything different."

According to Gill (GA), there was a progression as the group formed an identity, "The book and life made me angry. I wrote that in *my* margins. Then I used the questions to poke at what other people thought to see if we could really talk and not just be in class together."

One week into the project, it became evident that the student groups needed more space in which to connect and discuss. Beginning in week two, their structure grew to include two fifteen- to twenty-minute Google Hangouts per week. Here, each group connected to discuss their progress, the questions that they felt transcended their annotations, and current events that connected to their reading.

"Highlighting Doesn't Say Anything": Multimodal Affordances of Glose

The majority of student annotations were video posts despite the added step that required they record and post (for these classes through unlisted videos in YouTube) and embed that link into the book for shared viewing. When their teachers shared the numbers, students were surprised by their own volume and shared that viewing their peers' video posts was a significant trigger for their own rereading. Lys (PA) explained, "I read the book. Then I posted. Then I read what others posted. Then I went back to the book to see what I thought. So much reading and re-reading. And it made it better."

In exploring what it was that made video their preferred medium, both classes of students saw the same affordance—that video allowed them to be present within the text. Both teachers attributed the volume of video posts to students' use of smartphones outside of school. However, students identified as something more. Angel (GA) offered, "I don't read. But I saw myself reading here. And I saw other people use what I said to read . . . for real. . . . Video was the way to be a reader and to see the reading. Highlighting doesn't say anything."

GAINS, REFLECTION, AND NEXT STEPS

Both teachers identified several big gains that this project revealed, ranging from students' work toward rewriting their identities as readers to their sustained engagement across the five weeks, to their desire to now use video to capture reflection as they moved back to work with print texts. Where multiple possibilities existed for a summative assessment at the close of this unit, both classes of students culminated their study of *All American Boys* by writing reflective essays, which examined their reading processes and the big ideas they were taking away from their reading of the text. In these essays, they spoke to the importance of a current YA text, which presented what they identified as a necessary set of themes and issues.

Moreover, they spoke to how and where their reading was different—both in the use of Glose.com, the collaboration with peers, and the load that rereading presented. Students identified having a community of like readers present within the book was the essential draw, beyond the tools or modality. Where it mattered that they were collectively exploring a book that was urgently timely and about the cost of being a bystander, they cared most that they had a say in selecting it as their choice helped give agency to their discussion.

The gains for the teachers were reading-centric and pedagogical. Both spoke to their newfound understandings about what it meant to be a digital reader (or at least a reader of digital texts) as these were new skills for them to learn alongside their students. But, perhaps larger, they spoke of the importance of choosing to connect their students who struggle the most with literacy learning with both YA texts and opportunities to lever new technologies, which help to make reading visible, social, and even nonlinear. Ms. Hill explained, "I think of that class last when it comes to getting creative or using technology. I learned that my last needs to be first."

The challenge of any "pilot" of a new technology is to know where to grow it next, asking how and why. For both teachers, there was immediate recognition of this as a reading experience that needed to extend to other sections of classes, keeping the tenets of using a high-interest, complex, and relevant YA title and ensuring that students were collaborating with another group of readers who weren't physically present in the room.

Their thinking was also centered on continuing the growth of *these* students as rewriting an identity would take many more successes and scaffolding to move their skills from digital contexts to work with print text. At the center of their next steps were Taysha's (GA) words as she reflected on what was valuable about the project:

> I have been Quinn. Maybe I am Quinn. I see so much here at school and out there, and I feel my . . . my speaking up . . . bubbling up inside, wanting to come out. I yelled at Quinn when I read because he moved too slowly—but I'm the same. That's the point. . . . (Sighs.) I wish we read more that told it true like this does. And reading where I am in the margin. That way, you read me and you read the words. It's about more than the words, right?

Taysha's words remind us the power of digital reading that *is* multimodal, nonlinear, social, and marked with real purpose.

In conclusion, this project demonstrated that the practice of digital reading can no longer be one where students simply receive text that is presented to them on a screen. Instead, digital reading now is an opportunity to think around and within and beyond a text, mark up and annotate with multimodal tools, connect intertextually through hyperlinks, and sound their voice and ideas within a connected community of readers.

This is social digital reading, practices, and tasks that are driven by the reader and not by shiny tools or websites where this kind of reading might take place. Admittedly, these are new spaces for us as teachers, but when we open to learning alongside our students and exploring possibilities together, opportunities abound to do work that does real work.

REFERENCES

Bauerlein, M. 2011. "Too Dumb for Complex Texts?" *Educational Leadership* 68 (5): 28–33.

Beers, K., and R. Probst. 2012. *Notice and Note: Strategies for Close Reading*. Portsmouth, ME: Heinemann.

Jenkins, H., R. Purushotma, M. Weigel, K. Clinton, and A. J. Robison. 2009. *Confronting the Challenges of Participatory Culture: Media Education and the 21st Century*. Boston: MIT Press.

Kajder, S. 2010. *Adolescents and Digital Literacies*. Urbana, IL: National Council of Teachers of English.

Kajder, S., K. Turner, and T. Hicks. 2016. "Are We 'Reading Right'? Bringing Connected Reading Practices to the Classroom." *English in Texas* 45 (2): 5–11.

Kress, G. 2003. *Literacy in the New Media Age*. London: Routledge.

Leu, D., E. Forzani, and C. Kennedy. 2015. "Income Inequality and the Online Reading Gap." *The Reading Teacher* 68 (6): 422–27.

Wolf, M., and M. Barzillai. 2009. "The Importance of Deep Reading." *Educational Leadership* 66 (6): 32–37.

Chapter 2

Flipping the Teaching of Young Adult Literature with Preservice Teachers

Amy Piotrowski

Teachers today are expected to bring technology into their classroom to enhance instruction. Teacher education courses are introducing preservice teachers to methods of teaching with technology in order to prepare them for the demands of teaching in our digital age. One teaching method incorporating technology that can be used in secondary English classes, including lessons on young adult literature (YAL), is flipped learning.

When teacher educators bring technology and teaching methods that integrate technology into their courses, it can influence the ways preservice teachers plan on teaching in their future classrooms. Teacher educators would do well to consider how to introduce teaching methods that build a variety of literacy skills. Teacher education courses can introduce preservice teachers to new content, such as contemporary young adult novels, and to new teaching methods, such as flipped learning.

This chapter shares flipped lessons on young adult novels created by two preservice teachers enrolled in a course on YAL. These preservice teachers chose a young adult novel to read and then created a flipped lesson to share with the rest of the class. By creating this flipped lesson, the preservice teachers learned how to use technology to teach YAL.

REVIEW OF THE RELEVANT LITERATURE

Baker (2000) coined the term "flipped classroom" when he had his students read through his PowerPoint slides before class meetings so that class time could be spent applying the content. Former science teachers Bergmann and Sams (2014) say that flipped learning is a "flexible technique to be used when appropriate to maximize face-to-face time with students" (35). Flipped learning allows direct instruction to be offered as needed to individuals and small groups, often through digital video and other digital resources, instead of through lectures from the teacher to the whole class at the same time.

Flipped learning can facilitate student-centered, active methods such as project-based learning, as students can consult video lessons as needed while they work on projects and topics they find interesting. Since teachers can use a variety of technology tools to flip instruction, this method can be used; however, it best fits the needs of the teachers and students.

Previous research suggests that preservice teachers may best learn how to incorporate technology in content area methods courses, rather than educational technology courses outside of a content area (Keeler, 2008). Elliot-Johns (2017) argues that teacher educators, including teacher educators who teach courses in YAL, need "to find innovative ways of integrating technology into enhanced classroom practices" (41). Methods for teaching with technology can be part of preservice teachers' learning in a YAL course.

There is no published research specifically on using flipped learning to teach YAL. In their study of flipped learning, Piotrowski and Witte (2016) had participants who made flipped lessons on YAL, but YAL was not the focus of what this study's participants did. This chapter seeks to begin to address this lack of research by examining how preservice teachers flipped instruction on YAL in an English education course.

CONTEXT OF THE FLIPPED LESSON VIDEO PROJECT

The flipped lessons shared here were created by preservice teachers who took a course on teaching YAL. This course was offered through the English department of a land-grant research university in the United States. This section of the course was online and offered for preservice teachers taking courses through the university's distance education program.

The preservice teachers in this course read several young adult novels together and discussed these novels through an online discussion board. Discussions on the novels were done within small groups set up by the course instructor. The preservice teachers wrote an analysis of each novel that they read. Then, each member of the course chose a young adult novel to read on their own and made a flipped lesson video for that novel.

To get this flipped lesson project started, the preservice teachers in this course read Sams and Bergmann's (2013) article on how to flip instruction. They also had an introduction to flipped learning via a video lecture from the course instructor. Then preservice teachers discussed flipped learning and the Bergmann and Sams' article as part of their weekly discussion board.

The preservice teachers wrote a lesson plan for their flipped lesson that they then shared on the course discussion board. They created their flipped lesson videos and shared their video lesson with the rest of the course. The preservice teachers watched each other's flipped lesson videos and commented on the lessons. This gave members of the course the opportunity to get feedback from their peers.

At the end of the semester, the preservice teachers wrote a final reflection about what they learned during the course. They wrote about their flipped lessons, how they thought their lesson went, and how they could teach YAL in their future classrooms. The course encouraged the preservice teachers to think about the ways flipped lessons can be utilized to teach YAL.

For this chapter, the researcher looked at two preservice teachers' work in this course. The researcher collected these two preservice teachers' flipped lesson videos, discussion board posts, and final reflections. The two preservice teachers are here referred to by pseudonyms, Brian and Charlotte.

BRIAN: USING A FLIPPED LESSON TO DO TRADITIONAL LITERARY ANALYSIS

Brian made his flipped lesson on *Buried Onions* (2006) by Gary Soto. Soto's novel is about Eddie, a boy growing up in Fresno, California, who deals with poverty and the lures of gang life. Because so much of the novel centers on the character of Eddie, Brian's lesson was on character types. He wanted his students to be able to analyze the characters in the novel. Brian provided his students with a lesson that uses popular culture to get students prepared to write a traditional character analysis essay about a young adult novel.

Brian began his flipped lesson video by telling his students to pay attention to the types of characters found in the novel and how having different types of characters develops the plot. He gave his students definitions for different types of characters found in literature: dynamic, static, round, foil, protagonist, and antagonist. Then he explained how different characters in the novel are examples of these character types. He went over how Eddie is a dynamic character, Angel is a flat character, Jose and Eddie are round characters, and Mr. Styles is a static character. Brian also explained that Eddie is a protagonist with gang life as the antagonist.

In order to connect these character types to characters that students know from movies and other stories, Brian gave more examples of character types from popular culture. He explained that Ebenezer Scrooge is a dynamic character, the Orcs from *The Lord of the Rings* are flat characters, Cinderella's stepsisters are foils to her, Shrek is a round character, and Scar from *The Lion*

King is a static character. Brian also discussed how Batman and the Joker are a protagonist and antagonist. He also went over some stock characters, such as the jock and the math nerd.

Brian spent the next part of the video lesson going over the character analysis essay that students will write when they finish reading the novel. Students will choose a character from the novel to write about, developing a thesis statement and finding evidence to support their claims. The focus of the essay will be to explain the function the character has in the novel. Students' essays will have five paragraphs: an introductory paragraph with a thesis statement, three supporting paragraphs, and a conclusion.

To finish the video lesson, Brian provided four writing prompts for students to consider. These prompts were designed to get students to think about the material in the video lesson as well as prepare students for the character analysis essay they will write later. The prompts were:

- Thinking of your own life with you as the protagonist, can you think of anybody you know that could fulfill archetypal character roles?
- Can a story function without a dynamic character?
- Can the protagonist be a "bad" character?
- Choose a favorite book and identify at least three character types in that book.

Brian wrote in his final reflection that he liked using examples from movies and children's stories to illustrate different character types. He felt that a lesson on character types is important for students because "for a story to be effective, typically it must involve more than a single character type." He believed that for his students to understand the literature they read, they need to understand the types of characters that they encounter. Brian said that in the future, he would want to spend more time with his students on writing analytical essays because he thought analysis is an important skill that his students will need to develop.

CHARLOTTE: PERSONALIZING LEARNING THROUGH LITERATURE

Charlotte's flipped lesson was on Leigh Bardugo's fantasy novel *Shadow and Bone* (2013). This novel's heroine is Alina, an orphan, who may have a magic power that can save her war-torn land. Charlotte focused her lesson on a key aspect of the novel—Alina's relationship with her best friend, Mal. She had her students connect Alina and Mal's friendship with their own ideas about friendship. By doing so, Charlotte's lesson sought to personalize her students' learning by bringing in students' own thoughts and experiences.

At the beginning of the flipped lesson video, Charlotte introduced the novel by discussion on the book's Russian and Ukrainian influences. She then presented one of the novel's key themes, asking students, "Will you succumb to peer pressure or have courage to stand alone and be true to yourself?" This question then leads into Charlotte discussing the importance of having a good friend.

Charlotte asked students, "Have you ever had a friend who meant the world to you?" She discussed the importance of Alina and Mal's friendship in the novel and how one's choices shape not only the kind of person one is but also the kind of friend one is. In order to get into the choices Alina must make between good and evil, Charlotte read the poem "The Light in the Darkness" by Trevor Barlow. She told her students that the poem "reflects" the novel.

Charlotte then provided students with an anticipation guide—a series of statements for students to agree or disagree with. She told the students that the anticipation guide is meant to encourage debate and that they will revisit it after finishing the novel in order to "see if feelings change" about any of the statements. The four statements on the anticipation guide were as follows:

- When in danger, it is best to play it safe rather than take a risk.
- In a survival situation, one must make decisions that are best for themselves and those they love, even if harm may come to others as a result.
- If you disagree with the policy of those in power, it is better to remain silent than to speak out and risk punishment.
- Commitment to duty and honor should outweigh individual misgivings in times of moral crisis.

Charlotte finished the video lesson by giving students six writing prompts. She told students to respond to two of these prompts in order to be prepared for discussion in class. These prompts were meant to encourage students to think about friendship and about experiences they have had that relate to the novel. The prompts were as follows:

- Was there an incident that happened in your life that forever changed you? If so, tell me about it.
- Have you ever felt isolated and alone? How did you find your way through?
- Have you ever felt pressured by your peers?
- Describe the struggle between light and dark?
- Why might it be hard for someone like Alina, who was an orphan and had to fight for everything she has, to accept the luxurious life at the palace? Why might she question the motives of the people who live there?
- Who was a friend that has made a positive or negative impact on your life? How did you meet and how did they impact your life?

In her final reflection, Charlotte said she was happy with her flipped lesson and the novel she chose. She wrote that one of the things she liked about creating a lesson on this novel was that "the characters are easy to relate to." She also commented that "there is action, adventure, the characters have to make tough decisions, and there is an abundance of material that can spark debate on a variety of topics." Charlotte also said that she was especially pleased to find the Barlow's poem because it "pulled everything" together and inspired her to have students write about their feelings and experiences. She said that this kind of writing would make the novel "more meaningful" to students.

CONCLUSION

The flipped lessons created by these preservice teachers demonstrate that flipped learning can be used to teach young adult novels in a variety of ways. Flipped learning and YAL can be a way to engage students in traditional types of writing, such as writing an analytical essay. Using flipped learning as an engagement tool with this rich body of literature can also help students reflect on their experiences and make personal connections to what they read. Brian and Charlotte's different approaches to teaching YAL through flipped learning reinforce the Bergmann and Sams' (2014) view that flipped learning is a flexible method.

It will continue to be important for teacher education programs to teach preservice teachers about content, teaching, and technology integration. As Brian wrote in his final reflection, "The ideas and constraints about the way to teach and the materials that are taught are constantly evolving." He felt that he had learned about books and teaching methods that he didn't know before he took this course, leaving him prepared to evolve with the times.

Flipped learning can be used with YAL to engage students in literary analysis and to encourage students to make connections between literature and their lives. It is beneficial for preservice teachers to get experience with technology tools and teaching methods that utilize these tools. Courses on YAL can be places where new books, new teaching methods, and new technologies can come together to enrich the learning of future English teachers.

REFERENCES

Baker, J. W. 2000. *The "Classroom Flip": Using Web Course Management Tools to Become the Guide by the Side*. Paper presented at the 11th International Conference on College Teaching and Learning. Jacksonville, FL.

Bardugo, L. 2013. *Shadow and Bone*. New York: Square Fish.

Bergmann, J., and A. Sams. 2014. *Flipped Learning: Gateway to Student Engagement*. Eugene, OR: ISTE.

Elliot-Johns, S. E. 2017. "Literacy Teacher Education and the Teaching of Young Adult Literature: Perspectives on Research and Implications for Practice." In *Teaching Young Adult Literature Today: Insights, Considerations, and Perspectives for the Classroom Teacher*, edited by J. Hayn, J. Kaplan, and K. Clemmons, 27–45. Lanham, MD: Rowman & Littlefield.

Keeler, C. G. 2008. "When Curriculum and Technology Meet: Technology Integration in Methods Courses." *Journal of Computing in Teacher Education* 25 (1): 23–30.

Piotrowski, A., and S. Witte. 2016. "Flipped Learning and TPACK Construction in English Education." *International Journal of Technology in Teaching and Learning* 12 (1): 33–46.

Sams, A., and J. Bergmann. 2013. "Flip Your Students' Learning." *Educational Leadership* 70 (6): 16–20.

Soto, G. 2006. *Buried Onions*. New York: Houghton Mifflin Harcourt.

Chapter 3

Socratic Learning Conversations: Ancient Practice Meets New Technology

Jenny Cameron Paulsen and Matt Copeland

STATEMENT OF PROBLEM

Traditional classroom discourse is teacher centered: the teacher imparts the knowledge, asking questions, and, most often, answering them. Teachers, not students, determine the viability of answers, when they actually wait long enough for students to form and articulate thoughts. Teachers tend to do the most talking. How are students supposed to learn to discuss ideas effectively if they rarely speak in class?

Often what passes for class discussion is not dialogue; rather, it is nothing more than a thinly veiled lecture. The teacher is actively engaged and the students are passive. In one study of 1,151 classroom discussions in over 200 eighth- and ninth-grade classrooms, 93.31 percent were teacher centered. Of the 6.69 percent that included moments when students directed the conversation, those moments lasted for an average of fifteen seconds (Nystrand, Gamoran, Zeisler, and Long, 2003). Too often, discussion is used as way of *installing* "correct" answers in our students. True dialogue, however, is a different type of conversation, an authentic exchange of ideas.

To create the conditions for true dialogue, classroom teachers can leverage new technologies and the established practice of Socratic Circles to increase the engagement of all students in classroom conversation, while learning about critical social issues through young adult (YA) literature. In Mrs. Paulsen's ninth-grade classroom, Socratic Circles are the driving force for deliberating, in both verbal and written form, about YA literature as diverse as historical fiction *The Book Thief* (Zusak, 2006), realistic fiction *All American Boys* (Reynolds and Kiely, 2015), and the YA essay collection *The Girl Who Was on Fire: Your Favorite Authors on Suzanne Collins' Hunger Games Trilogy* (Wilson, 2011). Establishing the Socratic Circle protocol as a scaffold for conversational learning, and a technology backchannel for visualizing and tracking the learning over time, creates a safe space for freedom within form where students can find their voices—and, most importantly, find their voices valued.

THEORETICAL FRAMEWORK OR REVIEW OF THE RELEVANT LITERATURE

Since 2010, many of the focal points present in learning standards for English language arts have shifted nationally. With the publication of the Common Core State Standards, the goal, the metaphorical "finish line" if you will, has shifted from the skills and knowledge necessary to graduate from high school to the knowledge and skills necessary for college and career readiness. Accompanying this paradigm shift came a renewed interest and emphasis on close and critical reading, text complexity, and using textual evidence to support ideas and arguments.

Although these next-generation learning standards offer most of their detail in the areas of reading and writing, they are more explicit than many of their predecessors in emphasizing speaking and listening as a springboard between comprehending and critiquing texts and conveying meaning. Classroom discussion is often where students first formulate and articulate their ideas, where they present their arguments and piece together the evidence they need to support those arguments.

This might occur while discussing *The Book Thief* by Markus Zusak (2006). Students dug deep into the domino image on the cover, and subsequently posited theories about the symbolic meaning of the cover choice and its relationship to Death, the narrator of the text. In discussion, students analyze and synthesize what they are reading with their own ideas and the ideas of others creating both communal and personal meanings.

This need for discourse in the classroom, of course, is not new information to educators or educational researchers. In fact, two large, meta-analyses of research-supported practices for improving adolescent literacy included classroom discussion among their "Top 5" recommendations (Kamil, Borman, Dole, Kral, Salinger, and Torgesen, 2008; Torgesen et al., 2007). However, even what educators know about our students need is sometimes subverted by the pressures of time, curricular coverage, and—sometimes—classroom management.

In one survey of teacher perspectives on classroom pedagogy, 95 percent of English language arts teachers reported valuing peer discussion, yet only 33 percent of those same teachers regularly make time for such practices in their instruction (Commeyras and DeGroff, 1998). The reasons for that gap between philosophy and practice are multifaceted; however, they often revolve around professional anxiety. Teachers may fear not covering the required content, or that discussion might raise questions with no ready answers, or they may fear their skills as facilitators will not sustain the conversation.

The protocol of Socratic Circles creates student-centered dialogue in the classroom and alleviates the anxiety that leads many teachers to avoid or restrict discussion. Through structure and organization, students are able to focus on content, and the teacher is able to focus on facilitation. Once internalized, conversation flows in an organic, yet purposeful, manner. This real-world dialogue prepares students for future academic and social. A Socratic Circle strives to be "a collaborative quest for understanding . . . dedicated to achieving an enlarged understanding of a text, not merely ingesting it" (Gray, 1989, 17–18).

NARRATIVE OF CONTEXT

Mrs. Paulsen, a veteran teacher, sought to create this "collaborative quest for understanding" in her junior high English classroom. Mrs. Paulsen's ninth graders held a Socratic Circle over the second half of *The Book Thief* and color psychology research. As the second circle of the year, there was still the need for training and growth. Students were learning the process of Socratic Circles, to give constructive feedback to the inner circle and to set goals for future conversations. The seeds of excitement were planted, and students responded positively to both the content and the process of the conversations.

After both circles discussed color symbolism and which characters seemed to show affinity for which love language, the outer circle debriefed and set some goals for the next circle. The students returned to talking about the book in the last five minutes before the bell. Even the quiet ones who hadn't talked much during the "official" time spoke. They asked questions, listened to one another, referred to the text, and continued discussing their thoughts about Death's gender, how the book would be different without Death's bolded comments, about Rudy and Liesel (platonic or romantic) and Max and Liesel (siblings or soul mates).

They conducted class without the teacher. Of course, this is one of the primary goals of Socratic Circles over time: to turn the majority of control and direction of the conversation to students. However, this idea coming to reality so quickly in the school year was surprising. Mrs. Paulsen paid careful attention to their thoughts and contributions and continued to take notes amid the chatter. When the bell rang, the students collectively groaned. They were disappointed to leave. On a Friday afternoon.

Encouraged by their engagement, Mrs. Paulsen introduced her students to literary lenses theory, based on the work of Appleman (2009, 2015), specifically the gender lens with the video "Girl in a Country Song" by Maddie & Tae (2014). As the video ended, one girl, usually quiet though not shy, slapped her hand on the table and said, "Finally! Let's talk about objectification!" The class virtually exploded with banter about the expectations presented by society based on gender and sexuality. They were hooked!

They quieted when handed the essay "Team Katniss" from the excellent young adult collection *The Girl Who Was on Fire: Your Favorite Authors on Suzanne Collins' Hunger Games Trilogy* (Wilson, 2011). They dug into reading, questioning, and highlighting passages they wanted to share. The next day, they all came in on fire for discussion. "Mrs. Paulsen, I had ten passages I wanted to talk about just on the first page! I can't believe you only assigned three for the whole essay." "Can we get in the circle now?" "Can I be first?"

The "hot seat," where the outside circle can jump in on a question, was filled at all times. This time, girl after girl after girl jumped into the discussion. It was a remarkable power shift that threw the more vocal boys for a loop. The discussion of the article reframed the Peeta versus Gale love interest debate as marginal to conflict in the story: Katniss versus herself. In exploring the depths of Katniss as a character rather than a point on a love triangle, she is defined as a complex young woman struggling to find her own voice. As a result, the girls in the class embraced their voices.

There were passionate, yet considerate, discussions about the difference in media portrayal between a love triangle with two girls and a guy versus two guys and a girl. One student asked: How would the story be different if Katniss was a boy? One notable observation: The Careers would have assumed Katniss was a threat if she were male—that her motive for volunteering would come from skills and confidence rather than love. This idea, proposed by a thoughtful male athlete in the class, ignited some interesting talk about the societal origins, both real and imagined, of such an assumption.

Mrs. Paulsen noticed, however, that they did not get to the obvious contradiction presented by Peeta volunteering for Haymitch. In debriefing, she brought this example to their attention. And the conversation erupted again, focusing on Peeta's feminine versus masculine traits. The conversation ranged over a breadth and depth of territory difficult to cover with only teacher-made questions, allowing for occasional surprising ideas that may never have occurred to the teacher.

The students discussed Katniss' childhood, the influence of her parents, the hard shell she grew to parent Prim, how hard it is to survive the deaths of loved ones, whether it is better to outlive others or sacrifice yourself to save another, how Katniss and Liesel were alike as survivors, and how the essay suggests it was hard to know Katniss because we are limited to what she knows about herself as a first-person narrator. A favorite quote of the conversation came from a feisty girl: "Katniss is the kind of girl you wanna BE. She doesn't need some boy to rescue her. She's BA. Can I say that? I just did. Katniss. Is. B. A."

As the bell rang, the students had just pried up a new tile in the floor of the both the essay and the story as they considered how the movie might be different if Katniss' olive skin in the book wasn't "white-washed" or if the love triangle had LGBTQ characters. They lingered, chattering amid the controversy, and again had to be shooed out the door. On the last day of the week.

PRACTICAL METHODS/APPLICATION OF IDEA OR APPROACH

Socratic Circles are a protocol for facilitating student-led discussions that help develop skills in close reading, higher-order thinking, question formation, speaking and listening. Just as important, they also help strengthen a host of social and collaborative skills, immediately impacting the climate and culture of a classroom, and often serving as a springboard for student writing.

Within the protocol, students are divided into two concentric circles: an inner circle, that discusses the central text, question, or issue of focus; and an outer circle that observes, then provides feedback to the inner circle once the conversation is complete. This recurring cycle of conversation and feedback, where the teacher serves as a facilitator of conversation rather than a participant or director, allows students increased levels of voice, choice, and engagement in classroom learning.

But at the heart of any Socratic Circle—any classroom discourse, in fact—is some text or topic that focuses students' attention and provides connection to their lives and the world around them. In YA literature with its relatable characters, real-world contexts, and vivid storytelling, there is a wealth of rich material for students to encounter, encouraging discussion of a variety of issues central to their lives while simultaneously developing their skills as critical readers of literature.

When contemplating using technology to extend and enrich classroom conversation, there are many possibilities for student use in both the inner and outer circles throughout the Socratic Circles process. When students are creating dialogue around a particular text, they can use tools such as Edmodo, Today's Meet, and Schoology to create an online discussion board that can be used before, during, and after classroom discourse.

Before Socratic Circles, the online discussion board serves as a central location for students to record their thoughts and annotations about the text, noting their observations, their appreciations, and their questions about the text for all of their peers to see. In the spring, when reading the novel *All American Boys* by Kiely and Reynolds, students gathered their curiosity and confusion collectively on a discussion thread in Schoology, a learning management system (see Box 3.1).

It is clear from their questions that they are engaged in examining the events and characters from multiple perspectives, seeking to uncover motivations and make sense of their actions. Nearly all of their questions came up in discussion in some form, circling back most often to "Why? Why did Paul attack Rashad?" Some sample discussion board prompts used include following questions:

- What surprised or shocked you in the text? Why?
- How do media influence the events of the story? What evidence is there to support your position?
- What if. . . ?

In this way, students learn from one another before the verbal conversation begins. Students see where their ideas might converge or diverge with the ideas of others. They can think through how to respond if their ideas are challenged and what evidence to use to support their opinions and/or positions. The discussion board provides a written record of initial curiosity and confusion to which students can return as a checklist for their understanding.

Another prediscourse activity is for students to identify what they believe are potentially good opening questions to begin each inner circle. This practice has the double benefit of not only helping students plan responses to such questions but also offering students more voice in selecting the conversational entry-point rather than the teacher.

A third prediscourse activity, "buzzing," detailed in Copeland (2005) and Brookfield and Preskill (1999), is best described in a ninth-grade student's reflection on the importance of preparation prior to the circle:

> We did a lot of brainstorming activities before the Socratic circle so we were fully prepared for the final activity. I think the most helpful activity was when the class each got a note card and wrote down all of the questions that came to our mind. After we had written down all of the questions we put a star next to the best and most important questions. At the very end, all of us students took our note cards and we rotated around the room sharing our questions with our classmates. This was a good way to hear some questions that never came into our own personal heads.

After buzzing, many of those questions found their way to the discussion board as students felt more confident about their questions.

Likewise, students completing the role of the outside circle "observer" spend time on the digital discussion board during the discourse, recording what they would say if they were participating in the inner circle, adding questions and layers to the conversation. This role is the "Silent Contributor." Reading over the discussion board, a teacher can search for opportunities to dig deeper, push for textual evidence, and give formative feedback. The Silent Contributor thread is a permanent, interactive record of ongoing thought. As students grow and change in their thinking, they can visualize evidence of it in real time.

Certainly, students use the online discussion board after the conversation as well. The rich discussion created among students through Socratic Circles often carries beyond the class. With online discussion boards, students have the opportunity to return to lines of previous conversation, clarify their ideas, provide additional evidence and insight, synergize ideas into a more cohesive whole, and—at times—offer a mea culpa for their previous tone, attitude, and behavior, expanding both the academic and social/emotional learning of all students.

This interactive record also provides the opportunity to reflect upon class performance. Teachers and students suggest alternate strategies—including more voices in the conversation, being an effective leader, and supporting ideas with evidence from the text. This addition to discussion captures the most ethereal of thoughts and grounds student self-assessment in hard evidence. The notes of the other data gatherers on the outer circle (talk tally, text reference tally, discussion map), as well as the teacher notes, are also posted to the discussion board for student self-assessment reference. One serious young man summarizes his contributions:

> I think that I did well coming up with a few questions in my head before the discussion. I tried to talk occasionally, but not dominate the conversation. I did manage to reference the text once, and I also invited someone into the conversation. Overall, I believe that my active participation was very good.

He clearly recognizes the qualities of a strong discussion participant. Here, student learning transcends the conversation centered upon a particular text and takes on a long-term perspective building skills in speaking, listening, dialogue, and democracy.

Socratic Circles are never graded. Students do not ask how many points they've earned. They contribute and participate for the sheer engagement. They work for growth, not grades. They assess themselves with Copeland's discussion rubric and set goals for growth over time (2005). They reflect on their contributions, others' contributions, and our progress as a whole, with an emphasis on text reference support and encouraging others. The students can track growth through self-reflection on the extensive body of digital evidence. One example comes from a shy, introverted young lady:

> The most interesting topic I took away from the discussion was when S. asked, "If Rashad was female, would Paul still have beaten him?" This was a fascinating question to me because Paul was protecting a female in the first place. If the roles were switched, then I don't think Paul would have been as brutal as he was to Rashad.

CONCLUSION

Mrs. Paulsen has been using the Socratic Circle method of discussion in class for about three years; her understanding of the strategy continues to grow with every student conversation. In twenty-three years of teaching, however, no other strategy or structure has had the profound and immediate impact on teaching and learning in her classroom as Socratic Circles. Her classroom is alive with purpose and intent and anticipation for what's next.

So, what did it take to engage students and improve their learning? The answer is so simple, it's revolutionary: listen to their voices, verbally and digitally. Therefore, the impact of our Socratic Circles and YA literature—on democracy, classroom culture, and learning itself—is best articulated by the students' own voices. One girl wonders about the questions still lingering after the discussion of *All American Boys* (2015):

> I am still wondering about Rashad's drawings. I feel like, in the book, the author doesn't go over the drawings and Rashad's art as much as they could have. They did go over it a bit, but I feel like it could have maybe played a bigger part of the story. It also wasn't mentioned as much in the Socratic circles, either. Part of that is my fault for not thinking about it until now.

Long after the unit is over, the story is alive in her mind. She is still engaged with the text, the class, and the story. In considering the ultimate impact of Socratic Circles with online discussion boards, perhaps this young lady states it best: "You're not just reading the people who talk the most in class, and you're not just hearing the opinions of your discussion group. You're able to hear the opinions of everyone, which is kind of nice because you notice things you might not have."

Creating communal meaning, sparking new thoughts, and honoring all student voices in the learning process, aren't these the kinds of learning experiences teachers seek? For short-term impact and long-term growth over time, Socratic Circles with a digital discussion board capture the invisible golden threads of student thought which they can, through careful reflection, spin together into a collection of learning evidence, creating a visible record of their literate lives—their speaking, listening, and thinking about literature, media, and their world. One student concludes with the best description of the process that takes place in learning conversations: "It really pushes your boundaries and makes you think." That *is* authentic engagement.

BOX 3.1. ACTUAL QUESTIONS STUDENTS ASKED DURING SOCRATIC CIRCLE DISCUSSION

Actual Questions Students Asked during Socratic Circle Discussion of *All American Boys*

- What if Paul was black?
- What if Rashad and Quinn traded places? Would Rashad have helped Quinn?
- What would have happened if Quinn stopped Paul that night at Jerry's?
- What if the lady that tripped was black?
- If "Rashad is absent again today" wasn't written on the walls, would there have been as much buzz about it?
- What if they had security footage from the store?
- Why did Rashad say that he was ok with the protest when he really wasn't?
- What if Paul knew Rashad?
- What if Rashad had been wearing his ROTC uniform in the store?
- If you were in Quinn's place at Jerry's and seeing everything, would you do something to try to stop Paul or would you just leave it be? What would you do if you were Quinn, watching the whole scene happen?
- Do you think Quinn turned his back on Paul?
- What if Quinn was seen in the video at Jerry's? Do you think the story would have been different if Quinn had been in the video (on the news)?
- What would have happened if Paul had seen Quinn when Rashad was "stealing"?
- Why wouldn't Paul let the woman or Rashad talk about what happened?
- What made Paul touch Rashad in the first place? What was going on in Paul's head?

- What do you think could have been another factor besides color that made Paul beat up Rashad so violently?
- Why do you think the lady didn't get involved at all?
- Do you think Ms. Fitzgerald meant something when she said she brought all the chips except for plain?
- Where do you think Paul's racism stems from?
- Do you think Rashad and Quinn became more of friends at the end of the book?
- Why do you think Paul's family was so eager to defend him?
- Do you think Paul's family threw the party to mask how badly Paul screwed up, or do you think they were just ignorant and didn't really understand the situation enough?
- Do you think it was just mere luck that Rashad got beat up by Paul, and later found out his dad had wronged someone before as well, or did the author purposely put that in?
- What do you think is going on in the cover here?
- Do you think Guzzo thinks Paul did the right thing?
- Would a police officer really punish someone that badly for stealing a bag of chips?
- Do you think as soon as Paul saw Rashad walk into the store he wanted to find a reason to fight him?
- If Rashad was female would Paul still beaten him?

REFERENCES

Appleman, D. 2009. *Critical Encounters in High School English: Teaching Literary Theory to Adolescents*, 2nd ed. New York: Teachers College Press.

Brookfield, S. D., and S. Preskill. 1999. *Discussion as a Way of Teaching: Tools and Techniques for Democratic Classrooms*. San Francisco: Jossey-Bass.

Commeyras, M., and L. DeGroff. 1998. "Literacy Professionals' Perspectives on Professional Development and Pedagogy: A United States Survey." *Reading Research Quarterly* 33 (4): 434–72.

Copeland, M. 2005. *Socratic Circles: Fostering Critical and Creative Thinking in Middle and High School*. Portland, ME: Stenhouse.

Gray, D. 1989. "Putting Minds to Work: How to Use the Seminar Approach in the Classroom." *American Educator* 13 (3): 16–23.

Kamil, M. L., G. D. Borman, J. Dole, C. C. Kral, T. Salinger, and J. Torgesen. 2008. *Improving Adolescent Literacy: Effective Classroom and Intervention Practices: A Practice Guide* (NCEE #2008–4027). Washington, DC: National Center for Education Evaluation and Regional Assistance, Institute of Education Sciences, US Department of Education. http://ies.ed.gov/ncee/wwc. Accessed October 11, 2016.

Maddie & Tae. July 24, 2014. "Girl in a Country Song." https://www.youtube.com/watch?v=_MOavH-Eivw. Accessed November 7, 2014.

Nystrand, M., L. L. Wu, A. Gamoran, S. Zeisler, and D. A. Long. 2003. "Questions in Time: Investigating the Structure and Dynamics of Unfolding Classroom Discourse." *Discourse Processes* 35 (2): 135–96.

Reynolds, J., and B. Kiely. 2015. *All American Boys*. New York: Atheneum.

Torgesen, J. K., D. D. Houston, L. M. Rissman, S. M. Decker, G. Roberts, S. Vaughn, J. Wexler, D. J. Francis, M. O. Rivera, and N. Lesaux. 2007. *Academic Literacy Instruction for Adolescents: A Guidance Document from the Center on Instruction*. Portsmouth, NH: RMC Research Corporation, Center on Instruction.

Wilson, L. 2011. *The Girl Who Was on Fire: Your Favorite Authors on Suzanne Collins' Hunger Games Trilogy*. Dallas, TX: BenBella Books.

Zusak, M. 2006. *The Book Thief*. New York: Alfred A. Knopf.

Part II

SOCIAL ENGAGEMENT
Connecting Youth beyond School

Chapter 4

Responding to Young Adult Literature through Civic Engagement

Kristen Hawley Turner and Dawn Reed

Digital media has infiltrated every aspect of life. According to publications of the Pew Research Center, the majority of Americans use social media (Duggan, 2015). Teens, in particular, embrace Internet use, with 92 percent reporting that they go online daily and 71 percent engaging in more than one social media space (Lenhart, 2015). These digital habits bring opportunities and challenges for teachers of literacy.

On the one hand, students connect with others beyond the walls of the classroom in order to share—and develop—their views of the world. They can contribute in meaningful ways to society. On the other hand, teens need to develop skills of participation. They need to connect their academic lives to their social ones in productive ways. They do not necessarily develop these critical practices without the support of adult mentors. By rethinking the role of literature, particularly young adult literature (YAL), in English Language Arts (ELA) classrooms, teachers can help students use this literature as a springboard to civic engagement.

BRIDGING SOCIAL AND ACADEMIC LIFE

For decades, teachers have incorporated YAL into their curricula. In recent years, arguments for the value of YAL have focused on making reading relevant to teens' lives (Stallworth, 2006). We know that students are more engaged, more motivated, and more apt to read when they can connect to the text (Miller, 2009; Wilhelm, 1995).

Underscoring much of the conversation about relevance is a focus on traditional literary elements—especially plot, character, and setting (e.g., see Ivey and Johnston, 2013). Can the students relate to the story? Can they see themselves in the characters? Do they recognize the neighborhoods, geographies, and other descriptions?

In an age where adolescents have opportunities to connect with other readers digitally and to use their reading to spur their civic engagement, discussions of relevance must transcend the stories themselves. Relevance is about helping students to engage in conversations beyond the text, to participate in society through multiple means.

This chapter provides a new look at the meaning of *relevance* when discussing YAL. Specifically, it explores the question, "How do teachers engage students in conversations beyond the text, conversations that contribute to civic participation?"

Throughout this discussion, YAL is defined broadly as *texts* "either written for or read by YA readers" (Lesene, 2003, 54). Though Lesene used the term "books" in her definition, adolescents read digital texts daily, and these texts come in a variety of forms (Turner and Hicks, 2015).

THE NEED FOR CIVIC ENGAGEMENT

In *By Any Media Necessary: The New Youth Activism*, Jenkins, Sangita, Gamber-Thompson, Kligler-Vilenchik, and Zimmerman (2016) describe case studies that highlight youth engagement in participatory politics. The characteristics of such participation include the following points:

Circulation. In participatory politics, the flow of information is shaped by many in the broader community rather than by a small group of elites.
Dialogue and feedback. There is a high degree of dialogue among community members as well as a practice of weighing in on issues of public concern and on the decisions of civic and political leaders.
Production. Members not only circulate information but also create original content (e.g., a blog or video that has political intent or impact) that allows them to advance their perspectives.
Mobilization. Members of a community rally others to help accomplish civic or political goals.
Investigation. Members of a community actively pursue information about issues of public concern. (Jenkins et al., 2016)

The book itself explores "a core contradiction" of American society that, on one hand, government seems too big and too corrupt to be affected by individuals, yet, on the other hand, digital media allows "everyday people" the opportunity to engage (Jenkins et al., 2016). As users who participate in online spaces, adolescents have these opportunities literally at their fingertips via their mobile devices. Yet in order for students to be college- and career-ready, which includes being civically engaged, they must participate through careful, critical reading, research, and writing.

To achieve this level of participation, adolescents must develop agency, or "the capacity and propensity to take purposeful initiative" (Ferguson, Phillips, Rowley, and Friedlander, 2015, 1). This development of agency, which leads to civic engagement, depends upon individuals developing the literacies that enable participation. The ELA classroom can provide the kind of context that supports the development of literacies that allow for students to engage in a participatory culture. Their participation can be springboarded by YAL texts that deal with topics relevant to students' lives and contemporary civic issues.

A CONTEMPORARY ENGLISH CLASSROOM

Dawn teaches high school English in Okemos, Michigan. A believer in the power of YAL to engage students in developing a variety of literacies, Dawn offers students choice and the opportunity to build agency in their reading. She hopes that by participating in structured literature circles or less-structured book clubs or by reading independently, students will develop as readers, build understanding of traditional elements of a novel, become agents in their learning, and enjoy reading.

Additionally, Dawn challenges students to engage in conversations about the texts they read by inviting them to wrestle with contemporary issues in their own personal, academic, and civic lives. Dawn guides students to this kind of engagement by framing conversations about texts around essential questions (Smagorinsky, 2007) and encouraging explorations of relevant issues by engaging learners in their own inquiries. It is through this culture of inquiry that Dawn leads students to embrace reading as an opportunity to engage in civic discourse.

PRACTICAL APPLICATION: DEVELOPING CRITICAL DIALOGUE IN AN ELA CLASSROOM

To be civically engaged, students must develop skills that allow them to practice circulation, dialogue and feedback, production, mobilization, and investigation. Three of these areas can easily be a focus in any ELA classroom, regardless of the technology available on a day-to-day basis. YAL holds power to help students develop these necessary skills. The following examples, a composite of Dawn's teaching and her work with colleagues in the Red Cedar Writing Project, focus on developing students' abilities to engage in

- dialogue and feedback;
- investigation; and
- production.

These practices pair study of YAL texts such as *Monster*, *Seedfolks*, *The House on Mango Street*, *A Step from Heaven*, and *They Said She Was Crazy* with use of digital tools to develop these skills of civic engagement.

Dialogue and Feedback

In the media-rich lives of teenagers today, there is no shortage of controversy that can be discussed in an ELA classroom. Fostering learning communities open to discussing contemporary issues starts with creating an environment that honors and respects individuals and prompts questioning of texts, including the text of the world. By giving students space to dialogue about the social issues that affect them and to think deeply about these issues within the context of a particular text, Dawn engages her students through the use of essential questions.

One question "What is justice?" allowed students to move beyond the plot of their YAL text of focus: *Monster* by Walter Dean Myers. The goal was to guide students to explore issues relevant to the contemporary world and student lives, such as poverty, inequality, and restorative justice practices. Dawn wanted dialogue in her classroom, but she also wanted students to engage in the conversation globally; she wanted to help them understand their ability to provide feedback to others about the policies that shaped their worlds.

To practice the first skill—dialogue—the class began their inquiry with a four-corner debate, where students self-identified their levels of agreement (strongly agree, agree, disagree, or strongly disagree) with the following statements:

- Under our justice system, all citizens are treated fairly in our courts of law.
- Some words are so offensive that they should never be stated or written.
- Ideas of right and wrong are clearly defined.
- Nobody is all bad or all good.

After each statement, Dawn asked students to discuss their reasoning with the other individuals in their corner, and then each corner shared a summary of the group's thoughts. In this small group conversation, students used examples from current issues as evidence to support the position on each statement.

One issue that dominated the discussion was #BlackLivesMatter. Through the structured conversation of the four corners activity, students wrestled through ideas from the news, as well as their own experiences, about race issues in the United States, a topic that makes many uneasy. Students were able to dialogue within the confines of the classroom and support one another in constructing their own meaning about current events.

A Hispanic student shared that he had been called derogatory names by a stranger on the street. He used this personal example to articulate the fact that he struggled with the feeling that his race was not accepted by the larger society. His comment sparked further discussion among his classmates, who would likely not have talked so pointedly about the topic elsewhere.

Because the conversation was structured and completely student-driven, the teens were able to dialogue through their own experiences as they related to the essential question, "What is justice?" This kind of dialogue continued as the students read *Monster* and connected the plot to current events. For instance, Dawn shared a local newspaper article featuring a debate over whether or not a person was guilty of a crime related to murder, and the students discussed how they might engage in the conversation beyond the classroom, or, as Jenkins et al. (2016) might suggest, how they might provide feedback to those who determined guilt in this particular case.

Having developed this mindset of critical dialogue in her students, Dawn was able to introduce KQED Do Now (http://ww2.kqed.org/learning/category/do-now/), which invites students into weekly civics conversations. In this public space, teens engage as readers and writers with print and media resources, then join in conversations by posting comments on the articles they read or through various media, such as Twitter. By selecting Do Now entries that were related to the essential question under study, Dawn was able to encourage students to go beyond their reading of the class text and into civic engagement. For example, KQED has hosted the following Do Now topics that relate to the question, "What is justice?" which formed the inquiry surrounding *Monster*:

- What can today's social movements learn from the Black Panthers?
- Should members of a police force represent the larger population?
- Should athletes use their public platforms to make political statements?

Additionally, a search for #BlackLivesMatter on the KQED website produces several articles that invite student response. In order to scaffold students into this conversation, Dawn planned lessons on digital citizenship, professional digital footprints, and use of social media in professional learning spaces.

Dawn encouraged her students to continue their classroom dialogue in these public spaces connected to relevant world issues, so they might join the conversation and engage in professional learning with students across various spaces. In this way, Dawn helped her students to see their social media spaces as spaces of reading and writing (Turner and Hicks, 2017) and to participate critically in important conversations.

Investigation

At the heart of inquiry is an investigation, and YAL can serve as a springboard to developing skills of primary source investigation like interviewing and storytelling. Dawn has been inspired by her colleagues at the Red Cedar Writing Project at Michigan State University, who have successfully incorporated StoryCorps and Humans of New York into their classrooms. YAL can connect students to these kinds of civic engagements.

According to its website, "StoryCorps' mission is to preserve and share humanity's stories in order to build connections between people and create a more just and compassionate world" (StoryCorps, 2016). By collecting interviews with a range of individuals, the StoryCorps projects have increased understanding of marginalized people, helped connect people and create empathy, and engaged listeners in "thinking about how society could be improved" (StoryCorps, 2016).

Similarly, Humans of New York "provides a worldwide audience with daily glimpses into the lives of strangers on the streets of New York City" (Humans of New York, 2016) in an attempt to capture the stories—in this case via image and interview—of a variety of individuals. Both of these public projects have inspired teachers to have students interview people in their communities and curate their stories.

Connections to community emphasize the importance of being civically engaged and support teaching skills such as empathy and compassion as students consider others' perspectives. As teens record history and learn about others, they must practice skills of investigation and storytelling, and YAL in vignette form can support students' growth in these areas. YAL such as Paul Fleischman's *Seedfolks*, An Na's *A Step from Heaven*, and Sandra Cisneros' *The House on Mango Street* offer students models of characters who learn and grow from collecting other's stories, like that of the mission of StoryCorps and Humans of New York.

Investigation into character motivation can be accomplished through the use of dialogue journals that focus specifically on character actions and perspectives. For example, *Seedfolks* presents the stories of characters who separate themselves from one another based on race, religion, age, and life circumstances. These diverse individuals ultimately come together through their work on a community garden. As students read the vignettes, they can document stereotypes that are challenged when characters get to know an individual. Initially students can compile notes from the text and offer their thoughts on each character's perspective. Eventually, however, they can invite others to dialogue with them in shared journals.

In Dawn's class, student dialogue about these moments in the plot, as well as the students' investigation into character motivation, shifted to personal anecdotes. Conversations about bullying in school turned to discussion on violence in local communities. Without prompting, students questioned how they could make a difference and turned their reading of the YAL text into civic action.

A Step from Heaven and *The House on Mango Street* similarly offer content that can spur discourse around issues of community, race, and economics. Through story, the characters in these YAL selections highlight family experiences and the protagonist's identity within family and community structures. Conversation related to these texts includes investigation of the various spaces and places that impact characters' interactions with others. For instance, one of Dawn's students shared that reading these texts allowed her to think about moving from one country to another and how values—such as study habits and socializing—varied based on place.

By starting with investigation of the stories in the literature, students can build skills that support them in collecting, documenting, and sharing stories of individuals in their communities in the spirit of StoryCorps and Humans of New York. The skills of compassion and perspective will help to approach these tasks with a civic mind.

Production

In a digital world, production requires more traditional knowledge—genre, audience, context—as well as knowledge of technology, which can impact any of the other three (Hicks, Turner, and Stratton, 2013). In order to "create original content . . . that allows them to advance their perspectives" (Jenkins et al., 2016), students must first identify a perspective and then produce content that advances it. In Dawn's class, YAL serves as a bridge to production as civic engagement.

Kristine Brickey, a YAL author who lives near Dawn's school, visited Dawn's students to talk about her novel *They Said She Was Crazy*. In the text of this novel, the main character deals with losing her son to suicide. Though not autobiographical, the plot reflects the life of Brickey herself, who lost her own son to suicide. Brickey's writing allowed her to offer commentary on this very potent issue in society.

Hearing the author talk about her work shaped the way the students read the book, and Dawn pushed their engagement further by inviting them to create messages related to suicide prevention or another important world issue.

In the spirit of participatory engagement, she asked them to produce some form of media that could be shared beyond the classroom walls. Because of the topic of the shared reading, most students explored suicide prevention in their compositions; however, Dawn offered choice for students to engage in analysis of any issue of concern to them.

Annie and Ryan (pseudonyms) created a public service announcement to bring the issue of teen suicide to light. The task required the pair to articulate a claim (that teen suicide is a problem) and to find evidence to support that claim. They skillfully moved between images, like the one in Figure 4.1, and statistics to weave a compelling argument (Figure 4.2), one that encourages viewers to act in order to prevent teen suicides.

Turner and Hicks (2017) suggested that students must develop an understanding of the moves of argument in digital spaces in order to read and write digital texts critically and to contribute productively to public discourse. As teens in Dawn's class worked with digital media to extend their reading of *They Said She Was Crazy*, they developed their skills of digital argument even as they entered a conversation with a real-world audience. This conversation took place at Youth Voices (http://youthvoices.live),[1] where Annie and Ryan published their work in response to a "Raise Your Voices" prompt that invited students to create media responses to topics that inspired them. This contribution to the online discussion represented an act of civic engagement that originated with the teens' reading of a YAL text.

ADDITIONAL RESOURCES

Three of the five areas of the framework of participation outlined by Jenkins et al. (2016) provide clear access points in the ELA classroom. Articulating how YAL can serve as a bridge through those access points to civic participation expands the conversation of relevance in using YAL in the adolescent classroom.

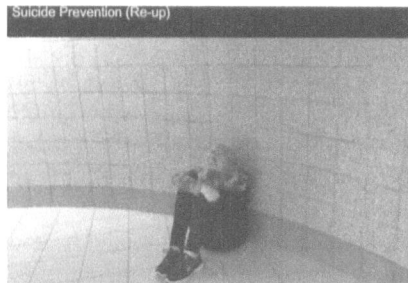

Figure 4.1. Image from the PSA

Figure 4.2. Statistic from the PSA

Some of the spaces mentioned in this chapter allow for students to develop skills associated with the final two areas of the framework: circulation and mobilization. Students in the Youth Voices community are participating in a professional learning network. This website offers opportunity for students to engage in discussion with their own threads and commenting to one another. It also offers opportunity for students to collaboratively annotate a text. Students also explore shared curriculum in the form of playlists (connected through https://www.lrng.org/), which includes a badging process for successful completion of the curriculum. Additionally, Youth Voices hosts YouthCast, which offers opportunity for classes across geographies to dialogue about big questions and ideas via a recorded webcast.

Schools across the country are participating in work on Youth Voices, which is grounded in not only powerful digital writing practices and purposeful technology integration but also shared community. This space supports students' voice through the very nature of the work and opportunity to write about civic issues. Additionally, Youth Voices connects work from various educational spaces, such as KQED Do Now.

In the fall of 2016, Letters to the Next President (https://letters2president.org/)—a project supported by KQED, National Writing Project, and Educator Innovator partners—offered the nation's youth a space to share their messages with the future President in a genre of their choosing. This work supported circulation of ideas and offered a space for students to engage in mobilization as they share their ideas with others. For Dawn's students, further extensions for mobilization of student work often begin in these kinds of digital spaces in support of the professional learning network and branches off into the local community.

CONCLUSION

YAL is relevant to students' lives, but its relevance lies more than in the traditional narrative elements of plot, character, setting, and theme. Rather, YAL can lead students to think about the world surrounding them and to participate broadly, beyond the walls of the school. It is through this civic engagement that students develop agency.

To move beyond the text, seeking relevance that fosters civic engagement, teachers can focus on building skills of participation: dialogue and feedback, investigation, production, circulation, and mobilization. The Internet offers plentiful spaces for students to engage, and educators can empower student voices, even while building literacy in an academic setting. YAL can serve as both foundation and springboard to this work.

NOTE

1. Youth Voices has moved from http://youthvoices.net, which is where Annie and Ryan's PSA is published.

REFERENCES

Duggan, M. 2015. "The Demographics of Social Media Users." http://www.pewinternet.org/2015/08/19/the-demographics-of-social-media-users/. Accessed October 5, 2016.

Ferguson, R. F., S. F. Phillips, J. F. S. Rowley, and J. W. Friedlander. October 2015. *The Influence of Teaching beyond Standardized Test Scores: Engagement, Mindsets, and Agency*. Cambridge, MA: The Achievement Gap Initiative at Harvard University. http://www.agi.harvard.edu/projects/TeachingandAgency.pdf.

Hicks, T., K. H. Turner, and J. Stratton. 2013. "Reimagining a Writer's Process through Digital Storytelling." *LEARNing Landscapes* 6 (2): 167–83.

Humans of New York. 2016. http://www.humansofnewyork.com/about.

Ivey, G., and P. H. Johnston. 2013. "Engagement with Young Adult Literature: Outcomes and Processes." *Reading Research Quarterly* 48 (3): 255–75.

Jenkins, H., K. Clinton, R. Purushotma, A. J. Robison, and M. Weigel. 2006. *Confronting the Challenges of Participatory Culture: Media Education for the 21st Century*. Chicago: The MacArthur Foundation. https://www.macfound.org/media/article_pdfs/JENKINS_WHITE_PAPER.PDF.

Jenkins, H., and W. Kelley, eds. 2013. *Reading in a Participatory Culture*. New York: Teachers College Press.

Jenkins, H., S. Sangita, L. Gamber-Thompson, N. Kligler-Vilenchik, and A. M. Zimmerman. 2016. *By Any Media Necessary: The New Youth Activism*. New York: New York University Press. Available at http://connectedyouth.nyupress.org/book/9781479899982/.

Lenhart, A. 2015. "Teens, Social Media & Technology Overview 2015." http://www.pewinternet.org/files/2015/04/PI_TeensandTech_Update2015_0409151.pdf. Accessed October 5, 2016.

Lesesne, T. 2003. *Making the Match: The Right Book for the Right Reader at the Right Time, Grades 4–12*. Portland, ME: Stenhouse.

Miller, D. 2009. *The Book Whisperer: Awakening the Inner Reader in Every Child*. San Francisco: Jossey-Bass. https://www.wiley.com/en-us/The+Book+Whisperer%3A+Awakening+the+Inner+Reader+in+Every+Child-p-9780470623428.

Smagorinsky, P. 2007. *Teaching English by Design: How to Create and Carry Out Instructional Units*. Portsmouth, NH: Heinemann.

Stallworth, J. B. 2006. "The Relevance of Young Adult Literature." *Educational Leadership* 63 (7): 59–63.

StoryCorps. 2016. https://storycorps.org/about/.
Turner, K. H., and T. Hicks. 2015. *Connected Reading: Teaching Adolescent Readers in a Digital Age*. Urbana, IL: NCTE.
———. 2017. *Argument in the Real World: Teaching Adolescents to Read and Write Digital Texts*. Portsmouth, NH: Heinemann.
Wilhelm, J. 1995. *"You Gotta Be the Book": Teaching Engaged and Reflective Reading with Adolescents*. New York: Teachers College.

Chapter 5

Social Media, Gaming, and Jay Gatsby: Integrating Youth Motifs with Youth Literacies in High School English

Alison Heron-Hruby, Lindsay Ellis Johnson, Dakoda Trenary, and Dallas Cox

Although publishers did not market *The Great Gatsby* for adolescents, English teachers have reconstructed the novel as a work of young adult (YA) literature by proliferating its core audiences, high school students. The novel is ripe for analysis from YA perspectives, including how adolescents use the social media and gaming platforms. The novel presents a quintessentially young outlook on life through motifs of infatuation and aspiration (Rimer, 2009). The novel inspired at least two works of YA fiction: *Great* (Benincasa, 2014) and *Jake Reinvented* (Korman, 2005), demonstrating that it lends well to twenty-first-century YA experiences.

The chapter provides a detailed description of how high school English teachers Dakoda, Lindsay, and Dallas collaborated to integrate students' multimedia preferences—including digital social networks and gaming platforms—into their students' study of the novel *The Great Gatsby*. These teachers polled their students about how they wanted to demonstrate their understanding of the novel as part of a new school initiative to include students' stated strengths in classroom learning.

The students' choices included Minecraft Mods and Sims worlds, particularly interesting because these platforms offered the students ways to reinterpret scenes and characters through visualization. Throughout the unit, the teachers also used mock ups of social media platforms, such as Twitter and Snapchat, to invite the students to interpret the novel through formats eminently familiar to them (e.g., tweets and status updates).

In particular, this chapter will demonstrate the value in having students use social media and gaming platforms as mediating tools for reading comprehension (Smagorinsky and O'Donnell-Allen, 1998). The guiding question for our chapter is relatedly: How can (and why should) high school teachers re-mix literary interpretation to include youth's preferred multiliteracies?

Samples of student work will delineate the unique and important contributions the students made through their social media and gaming activities to their class study of *The Great Gatsby*.

THE CHALLENGE

The teachers turned to the students' media preferences because they were concerned that the students would not give much thought to the novel, at least not in academically sanctioned ways. These students typically resisted reading silently; they preferred round-robin reading. In other words, many of them did not embrace reading as a solitary endeavor involving a single reader and a single text.

They wanted to read with their peers and teachers, but a paragraph-by-paragraph or page-by-page close reading had proven to prompt their surreptitious use of smartphones under their desks instead of an excitement for the dynamics of great literature. The teachers decided to try a different tack, one that involved the students' stated interests and talents, their predilection for shared reading, and their social media habits.

STUDENTS AS PRODUCERS

Their unit on *The Great Gatsby* was framed by cultural studies (Gemignani and Pena, 2007). To examine media use from a cultural studies perspective means to think about how users engage in both consumption and production of texts. Consumption involves using a text for its intended purpose, assuming the intention is decipherable. Consumption drives advertising, for example: advertisers develop a message about a product and try to control that message as much as possible so that their intended audience absorbs that message and acts accordingly (i.e., purchases the product or pays for its use).

English teachers, likewise, can approach reading as a process of delivering and understanding predetermined messages, one that involves close analyses of literature texts to uncover an inherent, explicit meaning put forth by an author. For example, the Common Core Standards for the English language arts contains the following directive for reading literature at the high school level: "Cite strong and thorough textual evidence to support analysis of what the text says explicitly as well as inferences drawn from the text" (National Governors Association Center for Best Practices and Council of Chief State School Officers, 2010).

When teachers treat students as producers instead of consumers, they demonstrate understanding that young people create, rather than absorb, meaning from texts. Cultural studies researchers, such as Henry Jenkins, have demonstrated that YAs can accomplish high creative and complex literacy endeavors if motivated to take an existing text and reimagine its contents by creating their own text.

The most well-known genre of text reimagination is perhaps fan-fiction, for which fans take the object of their fandom (e.g., the *Harry Potter* series) and compose new stories about the characters and settings. In their unit on *The Great Gatsby*, the teachers treated their eleventh-grade students as producers.

PIQUING STUDENT INTEREST

Rowan County Senior High School, where the unit featured in this chapter took place, is located in rural eastern Kentucky and has an enrollment of approximately 900 students. According to the school guidance office, the average percentage of students who pursue a postsecondary immediately after graduation is 70 percent; the average percentage of students attending a four-year college or university is 62 percent.

Lindsay's first time teaching *The Great Gatsby* in the spring of 2013—four years prior to the unit at the focus of the present chapter—was particularly special because the new film version starring Leonardo DiCaprio had its release date set for May. With its young star and a soundtrack by Jay-Z, the upcoming film made the novel an easy sell to sixteen-year-olds.

Lindsay and her English department colleagues at the time planned the unit on the novel to end right before the release of the film, and they worked with our local movie theater to take their students on a field trip to see it as a reward for finishing the unit. The millions of dollars spent advertising the film through movie trailers, clothing lines, and magazine covers seemed to be all the motivation the students needed to read. Jay Gatsby was "cool," and the students wanted to know why.

Lindsay and her students spent their class periods reading the novel, taking notes, completing reading comprehension quizzes, and discussing major moments in the plot—the same way she had read *The Great Gatsby* the first time as a junior in high school. The release of the film had made these traditional methods useful to the students in their quest to understand the novel in light of their interest in seeing the movie version, though Lindsay would find herself trying to recreate this intense interest repeatedly, each time relying on a current trend that offered little staying power.

Two years later, after the excitement over the new film version had died down, Lindsay discovered a new hook in the Trivia Crack game craze. It was the Sunday before the unit; she was playing her nightly round of Trivia Crack when it occurred to her the game could be her springboard for student engagement. Her students were as obsessed with the game as she was. Students would rush into her room and ask questions about authors or novels in order to beat their friends. Like Trivial Pursuit, Trivia Crack had color-coded categories in which students would be asked timed questions.

Lindsay spent the evening creating a unit structure for her students that tied the Common Core State Standards to the game, designating each color to a different aspect of studying literature, such as historical context, literary devices, and character dialect. The students were excited to use colors to gather and code important information. They loved the game-like fun of spinning a wheel to determine their color for the day. Lindsay deemed the unit a success. However, the next spring she ran into a familiar problem. Just like the excitement of the newer film version had worn off, so had the students' obsession with Trivia Crack.

Lindsay turned to her student teacher, Dakoda, and her colleague, Dallas, for ideas. She shared her Trivia Crack activity with them and her concern for how to make it "cool" for the 2016 group of kids. Dallas and Dakoda used essentially the same structure but based it on social media platforms instead of the Trivia Crack Categories.

True collaboration happened as result of Lindsay's request for help because all members involved were willing to brainstorm together, challenge each other, be creative, and put the work into making a unit that did not fit the traditional mold of teaching literature but did fit with the interests of their students.

This time the students did not read the entire novel during the unit because of time and homework policy restrictions: The teachers could not assign reading at home and could not spend more than three to four weeks on a novel without encroaching on other curricular demands, such as grammar instruction for the ACT. Therefore, they decided to show scenes from the 2013 film adaptation (Luhrmann, Martin, Wick, and Knapman, 2013) and from the 1974 film adaptation (Merrick, 1974) to replace about one-third of the chapters in the novel.

Ideally, the students would have read the entire novel because frequent and wide reading is vital to students' literacy development (Stanovich, Cunningham, and West, 1998). Yet, exposing students to the film scenes fits well within the multimedia approach outlined in this book because the students had an opportunity to experience the story in different ways—not just in print but also through the vision of two film directors, each with a unique approach (Simon, 2013). In keeping with optimal literacy practice of sustained, comprehensive reading, teachers could have students read the entire novel, using diverse visual media as interpretive tools.

STUDENT-CENTERED, MULTIMEDIA ASSESSMENTS

Because Lindsay, Dakoda, and Dallas were striving for a student-centered unit, it was imperative to ensure that the summative assessment was reflective of this intention. They agreed to give the students several options for the project format. As such, the students could choose the manifestation they believed best represented their mastery of the content covered during the unit, signified by their different and unique skill sets. In all, the teachers created a total of nine separate summative assessment project options. Furthermore, they divided the nine options into three separate categories: writing-based, presentation-based, and set-building.

Finally, to ensure that all nine options equated a similar expectation for work investment, they created a rubric for each of the three categories, each totaling 100 points possible. They ensured that each category rubric was applicable to the separate project options within the sections, and then explained the plethora of creative options to the students. The following is a synopsis of each of the three categories and their individual fulfillment expectations:

Writing-based: This category included three separate options. The teachers let the students know that whoever among them had anxiety concerning presenting in front of an audience needed to choose an option from this category, as it was the only one not required to present. The specific project options included the following:

- An in-depth essay comparing/contrasting the novel version to the movie version
- Song lyrics for an appropriate lyrical addition to the movie or novel, with a justification for its creation and choice of scene for addition
- A work of creative fiction functioning as an alternate ending to the general plot (may be in novel format or screenplay format).

Presentation-based: This category included two separate project options, both of which required a final presentation to the class:

- A presentation comparing the themes/events of the 1920s to modern-day equivalents
- A presentation of their original-body biography (see rubric).

It should also be noted that students were informed that presentations in this category must take the format of a PowerPoint, Prezi, infographic, video, or poster.

Set-building: This category included four separate project options, all of which required a final presentation to the class:

- A physically constructed setting as related to either descriptions in the novel or images from the movie
- A Minecraft, Sims, or other computer-generated model developed setting as related to either descriptions in the novel or images from the movie
- A cake or other personally made food constructed to represent a setting as related to either descriptions in the novel or images from the movie
- A video of a set you built (but for some reason cannot transport to class), which is important to the novel or movie.

Our fair warning: Some of our most creative projects came from the students who opted to bake a cake and construct decorations on it that were representative of a setting; however, for us, it ended with an abundance of cake to sample and eat!

Several of the students chose the option to construct a Minecraft or Sims model. Both platforms are games that allow players to construct their own worlds, either through building (in Minecraft) or through interpersonal relationships and city infrastructure (in Sims). The students who chose this option used their knowledge of character development or setting to construct their models.

Figure 5.1 shows a student-created model of Gatsby's mansion at night, awaiting party guests. The model demonstrates the student's understanding of the grandness of the mansion, the expansiveness of the lawn, and the role of lights in evening in the novel. All symbolize Jay Gatsby. To build such a model in Minecraft takes skill and patience; a player builds one block at a time and must understand scale and color tone to create the desired effect.

In addition to the summative project, students took notes every day in the form of "posting" to social media from the perspective of the characters in the novel. This task alone was challenging for a formative assessment, whether students realized it or not: they had to think from the perspective of a character and create new dialogue and interactions between the characters based on how the author developed them. The unit focused heavily on characterization and how it relates to plot and setting, so it only seemed fair to give the students as much perspective on these characters as possible.

They read about the characters as Fitzgerald portrayed them in the novel as well as see the two different takes on the characters as presented in the 1974 and 2013 films. Blending the two different mediums and three different perspectives in the classroom allowed the students to understand these characters from multiple vantage points and gave them creative freedom to reinvent these characters as modern-day Internet users.

Figure 5.1. Student's visual interpretation of Jay Gatsby's mansion

When students walked in for class, before anything else, they would look at the board to see what social media format they had been assigned that day. They quickly got in the routine of picking up a blank slip as well as any materials they may need to complete their present task. The response was thrilling. Students pulled in modern song lyrics that applied to the characters, trending hashtags, and portrayed the relationship between characters with likes, screenshots, and comments. They were painting a digital image of what the characters would look like if they were alive today.

Below is a sample template for the social media posts the students used for Gatsby:

Status Update

INSTRUCTIONS: Compose a status update related to an event in the novel, from your chosen character's point of view. If relevant, add hashtags to capture the tone or theme of the update: _____
_____
_____

Additional Resources

The following resources are helpful for creating a similar unit. Additionally, the books can help teachers articulate why a multimedia approach contributes to the rigor of a traditional literature curriculum.

Books

1. *What Video Games Have to Teach Us about Learning and Literacy* (Gee, 2014)
2. *Hanging Out, Messing Around, and Geeking Out: Kids Living and Learning with New Media* (Ito et al., 2009)

Websites

1. Project New Media Literacies: http://www.newmedialiteracies.org/teachers-strategy-guide/.
2. Media Education Lab: http://mediaeducationlab.com/ready-set-create-multimedia-authorship-101.

CONCLUSION

Overall, using gaming and social media during the unit on *The Great Gatsby* helped the students to tap into the "cool" factor of the novel, just as the release of the 2013 film had done for Lindsay's students four years earlier. While Lindsay, Dallas, and Dakoda know that they may have to change things up again to converge with students' most recent uses of and interests in digital technology, during the present unit, there were two notable differences from Lindsay's previous years' attempts.

The first difference was that at first, she and her colleagues Dallas and Dakoda designed an open-ended summative assessment dependent upon students' present interests and talents, a move that would allow them to adapt the assessment readily to future literature units.

The second notable difference surrounded collaboration. Entering into a collaboration with Dallas and Dakoda allowed her to adjust the unit from the previous year, energizing her and providing her the advantage of other teachers' perspectives. Coincidentally, the collaboration allowed her to mentor two new teachers. Although digital media and gaming were key to these teachers' reimagining of *The Great Gatsby*, their collaboration played a vital role, as well.

This unit reminded us that students are excellent creative thinkers when they are given the chance to showcase their talents and build on their existing literacies. Digital literacies, in particular, allowed the students to analyze the novel in ways that traditional formats, such as essays and teacher-directed class discussions, might not as easily foster.

For example, it would be difficult to capture the visual brilliance in Fitzgerald's novel without a visual rendering, and social media posts are uniquely appropriate for representing the social structures and mores that Fitzgerald portrays. We believe that young adults' digital proclivities are an especially excellent match for novels that feature visual metaphor and social structure.

REFERENCES

Benincasa, S. 2014. *Great*. New York: HarperTeen.

Gee, J. P. 2014. *What Video Games Have to Teach Us about Learning and Literacy*. New York: Macmillan.

Gemignani, M., and E. Peña. 2007. "Postmodern Conceptualizations of Culture in Social Constructionism and Cultural Studies." *Journal of Theoretical and Philosophical Psychology* 27 (2-1): 276.

Ito, M., S. Baumer, M. Bittanti, R. Cody, B. H. Stephenson, H. A. Horst, and D. Perkel. 2009. *Hanging Out, Messing Around, and Geeking Out: Kids Living and Learning with New Media*. Cambridge, MA: MIT Press.

Jenkins, H. 2006. *Convergence Culture: Where Old and New Media Collide*. New York: New York University Press.

Korman, B. 2005. *Jake, Reinvented*. New York: Hyperion.

Luhrmann, B., C. Martin, D. Wick, and C. Knapman, producers, and B. Luhrmann, director. 2013. *The Great Gatsby* [Motion picture]. United States: Warner Brothers.

Merrick, D., producer, and J. Clayton, director. 1974. *The Great Gatsby* [Motion picture]. United States: Paramount Pictures.

National Governors Association Center for Best Practices and Council of Chief State School Officers. 2010. *Common Core State Standards for English Language Arts and Literacy in History/Social Studies, Science, and Technical Subjects*. Washington, DC: Authors.

Rimer, S. November 7, 2009. "*The Great Gatsby* Resonates with Urban Adolescents." *New York Times*. http://www.nytimes.com/2008/02/17/world/americas/17iht-gatsby.1.10107935.html?_r=0.

Simon, S. May 4, 2013. "'The Great Gatsby': Retold Again with a Distinct Treatment." *National Public Radio Weekly Edition*. Radio broadcast. http://www.npr.org/2013/05/04/181053779/the-great-gatsby-retold-again-with-a-distinct-treatment.

Smagorinsky, P., and C. O'Donnell Allen. 1998. "Reading as Mediated and Mediating Action: Composing Meaning for Literature through Multimedia Interpretive Texts." *Reading Research Quarterly* 33 (2): 198–226.

Stanovich, K. E., A. E. Cunningham, and R. F. West. 1998. "Literacy Experiences and the Shaping of Cognition." In *Global Prospects for Education: Development, Culture, and Schooling*, edited by S. Paris and H. Wellman, 253–88. Washington, DC: American Psychological Association.

Chapter 6

Infusing Young Adult Literature into the Virtual Classroom

Brooke Eisenbach, Paula Greathouse, and Jennifer Farnham

Who could have ever imagined students would one day engage in classroom learning by logging into a computer? With the tap of a power button and click of a keyboard, students now have the opportunity to learn and engage with others from around the world. Virtual education is one of the fastest growing forms of school choice.

The National Education Policy Center (NEPC) published findings noting that as of 2014, there were more than 300 full-time virtual schools enrolling more than 200,000 students throughout the United States. In addition to the thirty states that host full-time virtual schools, even more states allow courses to be delivered through a hybrid classroom environment for public school students (NEPC, 2014). For the 2014–2015 school year, states' virtual courses served over 462,000 middle and secondary school students (Evergreen Education Group, 2015).

Middle and secondary students enrolling in today's virtual courses do so for a variety of reasons (Evergreen Education Group, 2015). For some students, logging into a virtual class is a necessary step in fulfilling a graduation requirement or simply a way to get ahead. Others find take virtual courses out of a physical, behavioral, or emotional need. For instance, some students sign in to virtual courses while undergoing treatment from behavioral treatment facilities, hospitals, or similar medical treatment facilities. Others take online courses while incarcerated in juvenile detention or in an effort to escape harassment or bullying in a traditional school setting.

No matter the reason, it is important virtual teachers find ways to address the needs of adolescent learners in this new educational platform. If anything, the current growth of online education, and the diverse student body signing into virtual courses, lends itself to the need for online curriculum and instruction that develops adolescent learner academics as well as social-emotional development.

WHY YA LITERATURE IN THE VIRTUAL CLASSROOM?

Virtual learning has the potential to isolate students. As they engage in asynchronous learning experiences, or log in to a synchronous session outside of their traditional school setting, there is potential they will become disengaged from academic or social conversation. As a growing body of diverse, adolescent learners sign in to virtual classrooms, it is essential that online educators uncover effective tools and strategies for engaging virtual learners in the reading, dialogue, and authentic engagement with young adult literature (YA literature) that supports content as well as the social-emotional needs of adolescent learners.

Twenty-first-century task demands require that students become literate beyond content. As virtual educators, it becomes imperative to include pedagogical approaches that allow adolescent learners to read, write, and discuss both the word and the world in an effort to promote equity, access, and opportunity. One way teachers can engage students in this exploration while developing content knowledge is through the inclusion of YA literature within their curriculums.

Adolescents live in fast-forward. Their bodies and minds are in constant motion. They are continually searching for answers to questions like *who am I?* and *where do I fit in*? They are critics, connoisseurs, and philosophers all rolled into one. As such, an educator with a finger on the pulse of today's adolescent understands the importance of including literature in the curriculum that challenges students to see their world in new and complex ways.

Young adult literature allows the adolescent reader to experience life's complexities vicariously in safe spaces, inviting them to self-explore and develop empathy. Given the diverse population of virtual students, the inclusion of YA literature in the virtual classroom offers these opportunities.

A large category of YA literature is characterized as realistic fiction positioned in worlds that reflect the complexities of adolescence. As such, teaching with YA literature is a key way of helping students develop intellectual curiosity, empathy, and a desire to improve their world (Wolk, 2009). Young adult literature has the power to transcend diverse perspectives and identities, which help adolescent learners better understand themselves and those around them. Furthermore, reading YA literature creates a safe space for adolescent readers, as they come to discover they are not alone in their experience and search for identity (Sokoll, 2013).

THE NEED FOR INTERACTION AND ENGAGEMENT WITH YA LITERATURE IN THE VIRTUAL CLASSROOM

As teachers plan pedagogical approaches to reading YA literature in the virtual classroom, it is important to consider the adolescent and the attributes and characteristics they possess that promote learning. Adolescents by nature are social beings, making interaction and communication key aspects of learning. Yet, the often asynchronous nature of the virtual classroom carries with it potential to engage reading as an isolated event, rather than as a social transaction.

Methods of community building within the online classroom differ from that of the brick-and-mortar environment. Instead of engaging with one another in a face-to-face setting, virtual students often communicate through synchronous and asynchronous channels such as web conferencing, phone, e-mail, discussion board postings, instant messaging, text messaging, and social media tools. Students might log in to a course at varying hours of the day or week in differing time zones. Often separated by time and space, virtual teachers encounter a greater degree of difficulty in connecting, engaging, and communicating with students.

Thankfully, research in virtual education points to the growth and development of new, inclusive means of fostering student interaction (Beldarrain, 2006). Adolescent readers can utilize new technologies, and teachers can implement a diverse array of instructional strategies in the reading, discussion, and analysis of texts. Virtual teachers are turning toward a variety of social outlets, applications, and collaborative tools as a means of enhancing students' critical thinking and collaboration. Though separated by time and space, it's entirely possible for online teachers to utilize strategies that actively encourage student learning and engagement with YA literature.

BRINGING YA LITERATURE INTO THE VIRTUAL CLASSROOM

Virtual teachers serve an important role in identifying potential titles for online learners and in encouraging student enthusiasm regarding textual choice and selection. However, the virtual classroom has potential to limit a teacher's opportunity to acquire information from colleagues and media specialists regarding popular titles and recent publications. The lack of a physical classroom space keeps teachers from sauntering classroom to classroom, or from making a quick trip to the library in search of the right book.

It is important that virtual educators utilize online resources to stay abreast of what is happening within the world of YA literature. Organizations such as National Council for Teachers of English (NCTE), Assembly on Literature for Adolescents (ALAN), and Young Adult Library Services Association (YALSA) provide virtual teachers and students the opportunity to learn more about popular titles, YA literature synopsis, and reader reviews.

Matchmaker, Matchmaker, Make Me a Match!

Once the virtual teacher becomes familiar with contemporary YA literature, it is time to learn more about the students in an effort to make the perfect match (Lesesne, 2003). In addition to personal communication and conversation, teachers can initiate a survey for virtual students as a means of gauging student interests, reading history, and current reading habits. For example, Janet Allen's (2000) Reading Writing survey or Donalyn Miller's (2009) Reading Interest-A-Lyzer survey is a great place to start.

Students can complete the survey via Google Forms, SurveyMonkey, or another online survey platform to share their interests. Even better, teachers can utilize conversational platforms such as Voice Thread to provide students opportunity to share their responses in a video or audio form. Teachers can then reply to student ideas with their own video or audio comments, thereby promoting discussion of student interests and selected YA titles.

Teachers can then utilize the online survey responses as a means of connecting students with an ideal text. In addition, the data analysis opportunities available through such applications can provide teachers insight into reading trends taking shape within their virtual classrooms. In this way, teachers can share out titles that might be of interest to a diverse array of students and further entice young readers.

Mini-book talks are another way virtual teachers can help connect the right student to the right book. Similar to book talks within the traditional classroom, quick, engaging talks serve as a means of inciting curiosity regarding a selected title. Virtual teachers can create a video presentation depicting images that coordinate with the book and discussing highlights or a preview of each novel. Or, for added effect, virtual teachers can solicit students to create and post individual books talks to share with their virtual classmates. Audio and video apps such as Animoto, AudioBoo, or Storybird offer valuable resources for this purpose (see Figure 6.1).

Though teachers hope students are able to identify books that engage and motivate them on an intrinsic level, it is not uncommon for traditional and virtual educators to find they are limited in their ability to offer student choice regarding book selection. Curriculum mandates or prescribed lessons can require students to read a predetermined text. If students cannot choose

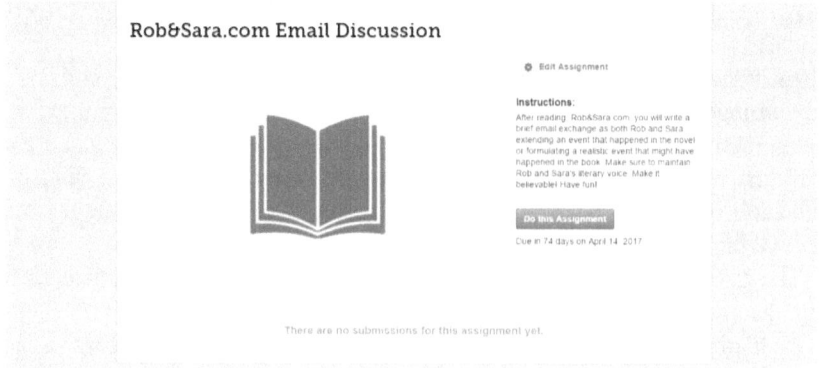

Figure 6.1. Storybird (storybird.com) screenshot
Credit Line: storybird.com

a novel because the virtual curriculum is unalterable, virtual teachers must strive to reach out to each student and get them enthusiastic about a book.

A teacher-generated book talk can provide a visual preview, along with images and a voice-over to highlight the novel and bring the text to life. In addition, scheduling a series of book talks or small group interactions allows students opportunity to interact with one another as they read the book. After all, adolescents crave social interaction and the online classroom can be a lonely place if students are not given ample opportunities to interact with peers.

Let's Chat about Books!

Reading is not an isolated event. Rather, it is intended as an interaction between the reader and the text in a particular context with a specific purpose (Rosenblatt, 1978). Even more importantly, reading is viewed as social event during which readers have opportunity to hear the voices of diversity and alternative perspectives. As such, it is essential that virtual teachers find ways of encouraging student to student dialogue within the virtual classroom. There are distinct ways virtual educators can accomplish this goal—whether they are teaching within a synchronous or an asynchronous setting.

One way to further student excitement and anticipation for YA literature is through an online literature circle. Teachers would need to arrange a live, online session at a designated time within a virtual classroom platform to engage students in book previews, discussion, and opportunity to offer advice for those seeking an engaging novel. Literature circles are a powerful way to engage students in discussion and can easily be adapted from the brick-and-mortar classroom to the virtual environment.

An ideal YA novel for selection for a literature circle is *Rob&Sara.com* (2004) by P. J. Peterson and Ivy Ruckman. The novel focuses on Rob, an affluent teen from a dysfunctional family, who breaks the law and ends up in a boarding/rehabilitation center, and Sara, a self-identified military brat, who loves poetry and desires above all to be a normal teen living in one place. Rob and Sara meet in an online forum for adolescent poets and their friendship, and later romance, blossoms throughout a series of e-mail exchanges over several months.

The novel deals with themes of trust and identity and the authentic connection that evolves in a virtual environment. They connect through the struggles in each other's lives and slowly start to reveal more about themselves in each communication.

After students have completed reading this novel, the teacher would need to hold a brief meeting online in a virtual platform, such as Google Hangouts, Blackboard Collaborate, and Facebook. The teacher could ask students following questions: "Is it possible to create an authentic relationship when you don't meet in person?" How do Rob and Sara use technology to connect?" What are some limitations of an online friendship?" "How does their relationship evolve?"

Students would participate in the discussion via the microphone or chat box. This is an important step to generate ideas about the novel that will help deepen the level of discussion. Next, the teacher distributes, or allows students to select, literature circle roles. Such roles might include facilitator (student who formulates discussion questions, oversees and moderates the discussion), illustrator/designer (student who draws or locates symbols/images from the book and types out captions), vocabulary seeker (must select challenging words from the text to define), and synthesizer (must make real-world connections) (Daniels, 2002).

Once roles are assigned, students are provided adequate time to prepare for discussion. At a designated time, they log in to the designated virtual platform to conduct their literature circle discussion. In utilizing a platform such as Blackboard Collaborate, the teacher can create a separate virtual meeting room for each small, literature circle group.

The teacher can rotate from room to room observing students and offering feedback or guidance as needed. If a student is unable to attend the synchronous session, but would like to learn more regarding the discussion that took place, platforms such as Blackboard Collaborate offer a recording feature, and other platforms, such as Facebook discussions, are automatically stored for later viewing. Students can submit a follow-up reflection, offering a summary of the literature circle discussion, additional thoughts on the novel, and feedback concerning what they learned from their peers.

Easy to create and access from anywhere, blogging can be another medium through which virtual students discuss their reading of YA literature. Denise Vega's *Click Here (To Find Out How I Survived the Seventh Grade)* (2005) is a contemporary middle-level novel focused on the experiences of twelve-year-old Erin Swift as she navigates her way through her first year at Molly Brown Middle School.

Throughout the novel, Erin shares her day-to-day interactions with teachers, friends, and enemies in the form of personal blog posts. She has a personal passion for web design, and utilizes this passion in working with classmates to create a school-wide intranet broadcast. Although her blog is intended to be a private space in which she can share the highs and lows of middle school life and relationships, things go awry when her innermost thoughts are broadcast for the entire school to see.

There is a wide array of ways teachers can infuse Vega's novel and online blogging in the virtual classroom. For instance, just as Erin reflected on her life in a personal blog journal, as students engage in reading and discussing the novel, they can reflect on personal connections and interpretations within their own personal blog journal.

Virtual students can also be charged with creating a personal blog page that records their individual interactions with the text. Included on each blog page can be visuals, hyperlinks to resources, music, videos, and so forth, which offer readers insight into the blogger's connection with the text as well as information about the text itself.

If crafted in teams or as a whole class, students can collaborate in the creation of a blog page showcasing their shared experiences as readers or learners. In the novel, Erin assisted classmates in learning more about coding and web design as they worked together to create and publish an online school news page. In branching off of this idea, and applying it to the virtual classroom, teachers can work with students as they collaborate together on a class or school-wide blog. This gives students an opportunity to draw personal connections to middle school life and utilize the text and tools for real-world application.

These ideas then become a starting point for conversations surrounding central themes from the text, as well as an opportunity to share their own experiences and school news with their community. No matter the approach, blogging as a tool for discussion and sharing provides students opportunity to develop skills in analysis and critique and engage a text in a real-world application.

Finally, there is incredible value in encouraging critical literacy within the virtual classroom. Given the context of the classroom and the characteristics of the online learner, reading YA literature that includes a focus on the influence and impact of technology can spark interesting conversations. Virtual Socratic seminars offer students opportunity to engage in critical discussions and examinations of these topics. While it might seem challenging, or even intimidating, to approach a Socratic seminar within the virtual setting, online platforms can be incredibly conducive to achieving this feat.

Feed (2012) by M. T. Anderson is set in a dystopian world inundated by technology. Titus, a typical teenager, and his friends must contend with the "feed" implanted in their brains. The "feed" provides a constant connection to the Internet. It draws on thoughts and emotions as a way to control. The consequence, people are losing the ability to think for themselves. While intended to make life easier, everyone does not welcome the "feed." As virtual students traverse this text and map character's reactions, thoughts, and feelings about the "feed," teachers can use the Zoom app as a platform for conducting a Socratic seminar.

Since the text is sectioned into four parts (Moon, Eden, Utopia, Slumberland), students have an opportunity to collaborate with most, if not all, of their classmates, as a Socratic seminar can be conducted for each section. A team of students meet in Zoom and record their inner discussion. Since this discussion should be student-led, the teacher can approach it in one of two ways. First, the teacher can pose an opening prompt to begin the discussion, and then allow for students to build off that prompt to continue dialogue. For example, in Eden, a teacher might ask students to respond to the following quote:

> They're also waiting to make you want things. Everything we've grown up with . . . it's all streamlining our personalities so we're easier to sell to . . . they do these demographic studies that divide everyone up into a few personality types, and then you get ads based on what you're supposedly like. They try to figure out who you are, and to make you conform to one of their types for easy marketing. (80–81)

The teacher could ask students to begin their discussion by describe the marketing techniques used in both the text and on social media sites, such as Facebook. The teacher could also ask the students to describe what types of ads they would have if they had the "feed." Or, the teacher might assign a student to be the discussion leader, or require each student to bring one open-ended question to ask during the seminar. No matter the approach, after the recording of the inner circle is complete, a second group of students will watch the video, at the same designated time—and communicate through a written discussion regarding their thoughts, questions, and critical considerations of the conversation.

The teams then switch roles, and complete the same process, until all parts of the book have been read and discussed. The task ends with a written reflective piece from each student discussing his or her beliefs about the role and use of technology in our everyday lives. Some prompts that a teacher could pose to guide this discussion could be as follows:

- The author dedicates his book "to all those who resist the feed." What does he mean?
- Describe the role of technology in the story.
- What role does technology play in your world?
- Drawing on evidence from the text, discuss potential benefits and consequences of the advancement of technology in our society.

Through the use of this digital tool, students are able to collaborate and critically reflect on their interpretations of this YA novel.

Sharing Ideas with the World

A final component of engaging virtual learners in the fascinating world of YA literature is providing them opportunity to share their newfound text and interpretations with those outside the classroom. A key advantage to learning online is immediate access to a worldwide audience. Project presentations carry a new meaning. Rather than standing in front of the classroom, sharing their understanding and achievements with the thirty or so students in attendance, virtual learners can complete projects and activities that speak across international lines—to an audience more diverse than we might have ever imagined!

One such project ideas is a student wiki, a collaborative website and useful tool to discuss and share YA literature in a virtual classroom setting. Students can work independently, or collaboratively. Students have the autonomy to decide when and how to "meet": such as a virtual medium, online chat such as Skype IM and conference call, texting, and even through traditional phone calls. The teacher can act as a facilitator, providing students a guide or template for their wiki: title, author, synopsis, literary terms identified, motifs, and themes. Students assume responsibilities for the wiki including the task of editing the site for online publication.

The benefits to this project are numerous: the students discuss and collaborate on ideas, use technology to create an aesthetically appealing page, learn how to edit and revise their own work, and create a final publishable product. Students can also allow their classmates to comment on different pages on the wiki to further allow for feedback and outreach of one another's work.

Most young adults and teens are heavily engaged in social media and social apps in the twenty-first century. As such, social media lends itself very naturally to student-generated mini-projects that promote instant discourse with a social media audience. On social media sites, such as Facebook or Twitter, the student, or teacher, acts as facilitator and poses critical discussion-based questions.

Virtual classmates can provide instant feedback and commentary regarding student suggestions and ideas. In addition, students can infuse images and student-generated videos to illustrate key concepts or critical interpretations of a novel. Polling features further prompt students to ask questions and generate further discussion of a text.

The virtual teacher can evaluate students' learning based on the quality and commentary occurring in the discussion and offer feedback to students along the way. Social media outlets such as Instagram, where pictures and videos are the central focus, present an opportunity for students to engage in a visual pictorial of their novel with captions for added commentary.

On Twitter, students can write out 140-character sentences and also attach pictures or videos. Similar to the Instagram storytelling described earlier, Twitter can be used to also tell a story in idea increments. Students can utilize thematic hashtags, or use the novel title, for added feedback through a wider social media audience.

Rachel Vail's middle-grade novel *Unfriended* (2014) weaves reference to a variety of social media tools throughout the narratives of a group of eighth-grade friends. This novel, told from multiple perspectives—each chapter providing a different point of view for the reader to consider—centers around relationships and conflicts that arise as a circle of friends navigate their way through the middle school social scene.

Throughout the story, the characters reference and engage in social media apps as they strive to understand who they can trust, and who they should "unfriend." As they post, tag, and reply to the photos and stories shared by one another, they begin to fabricate circumstances and events, causing a rift within the very foundation of their social circle. This novel not only lends itself to engaging with social media outlets in class lessons and activities but also encourages critical discussion of the potential dangers and pitfalls in placing heavy emphasis on such applications—a discussion warranted in today's middle and high school classrooms.

ADDITIONAL RESOURCES

When teachers include texts in the curriculum that reflect the real world of adolescents, they make literature relevant to their students. By providing students opportunities to discuss what they are reading, teachers enhance their students' critical literacy. In an effort to address this in a virtual classroom, educators must begin to make purposeful and intentional decisions about the technological applications students use in their reading and discussion of YA literature.

These decisions can be a scary endeavor on two fronts. First, the inclusion of YA literature itself may be a new undertaking. There are several resources available to teachers when deciding on which YA novel(s) to include. The Young Adult Library Services Association offers not only booklists to teachers but also a free app for students called YALSA's Teen Book Finder that connects adolescents with YA literature.

Journals such as *Voices from the Middle*, *English Journal*, *School Library Journal*, and *ALAN Review* are also great resources in locating YA texts. Both teachers and students can visit websites such as TeenReads.com and Goodreads.com to see what readers think about specific YA novels.

Some collaborative and interactive technological approaches may be unchartered territory for teachers. But teachers can't be afraid to try something new. Virtual learners deserve access to tasks that allow for authentic experiences with YA literature, ones that hold the potential to increase their engagement and encourage communication and interaction while allowing them to explore both the word and the world.

Online programs such as Skype, Blackboard Collaborate, and Google Hangouts provide a platform in which virtual teachers and students can meet together, chat, and engage in the reading of YA literature. Apps such as Edublog, Kidblog, and Wordpress offer free, safe, secure blogging publishing platforms. Lastly, The English Companion Ning offers a social network for online resources in reading and engaging in YA literature.

BRINGING IT ALL TOGETHER

Virtual education is expanding. With this ever-growing form of education come challenge and opportunity. All too often, virtual education has focused on methods of communication and collaboration that have the potential to fall short of achieving the same level of engagement and critical thought as instructional methods employed within the brick-and-mortar classroom.

The diverse population within the online classroom calls for attention to addressing the unique needs of adolescent virtual learners. Teachers must find ways of meeting the academic, as well as social and emotional needs of students, no matter the learning context. Reading young adult literature in the virtual classroom helps virtual teachers accomplish this goal. It is important to encourage virtual adolescent learners in their critical reading and engagement with the world of YA literature through today's virtual channels in an effort to help them see the importance of reading in their lives and allow students to grow and develop as avid readers and connoisseurs of young adult literature.

Throughout this chapter, we have highlighted particular texts and activities that blend the power of YA literature and digital capabilities in an effort to offer opportunity to engage and motivate virtual adolescent learners. Having students read and discuss texts such as *Feed*, *Rob&sara.com*, *Unfriended*, and *Click Here (To Find Out How I Survived the Seventh Grade)* not only allows them to relate to characters and situations that speak to their own experiences with social media and digital literacies, but also engages them in activities that utilize today's digital technologies.

Infusing a key focus on young adult literature within the online curriculum provides a safe space for students to explore their own identities while providing opportunity for peer-to-peer collaboration and community development. The inclusion of texts that speak to the individual learner, and activities that further opportunity for student engagement and dialogue, promotes connection, engagement, and student motivation in what might otherwise be an isolated learning event.

REFERENCES

Allen, J. 2000. *Yellow Brick Roads: Shared and Guided Paths to Independent Reading 4–12*. Portland, ME: Stenhouse Publishers.

Anderson, M. T. 2012. *Feed*. Cambridge, MA: Candlewick Press.

Beldarrain, Y. 2006. "Distance Education Trends: Integrating New Technologies to Foster Student Interaction and Collaboration." *Distance Education* 27 (2): 139–53.

Daniels, H. 2002. *Literature Circles: Voice and Choice in Book Clubs and Reading Groups*. Portland, ME: Stenhouse Publishers.

Evergreen Education Group. 2015. *Keeping Pace with K–12 Online and Blended Learning: An Annual Review of Policy and Practice*, 12th ed. iNACOL website. http://www.kpk12.com/wp-content/uploads/Evergreen_KeepingPace_2015.pdf.

Lesesne, T. 2003. *Making the Match: The Right Book for the Right Reader at the Right Time: Grades 4–12*. Portland, ME: Stenhouse Publishers.

Miller, D. 2009. *The Book Whisperer: Awakening the Inner Reader in Every Child*. San Francisco: Jossey-Bass.

National Education Policy Center. 2014. *Virtual Schools in the U.S. 2014: Politics, Performance, Policy, and Research Evidence. Section III: Full-time Virtual Schools: Enrollment, Student Characteristics, and Performance*. Boulder, CO: Miron, G., Gulosino, C., & Horvitz, B.

Peterson, P., and I. Ruckman. 2004. *Rob&sara.com*. New York: Laurel Leaf.

Rosenblatt, L. M. 1978. *The Reader, the Text, the Poem: The Transactional Theory of Literary Work*. Carbondale: Southern Illinois University Press.

Sokoll, T. 2013. "Representations of Trans Youth in Young Adult Literature: A Report and a Suggestion." *Young Adult Library Services* 11 (4): 23–26.

Vail, R. 2014. *Unfriended*. New York: Penguin Group.

Vega, D. 2005. *Click Here (To Find Out How I Survived the Seventh Grade)*. New York: Little, Brown and Company.

Wolk, S. 2009. "Reading for a Better World: Teaching for Social Responsibility with Young Adult Literature." *Journal of Adolescent and Adult Literacy* 52 (8): 664–73.

Part III

CRITICAL INQUIRY
Digging Deeper with Young Adult Literature

Chapter 7

Emerging Media, Evolving Engagement: Expanding Teachers' Repertoires of Young Adult Literary Study and Response

Anna Smith and Robyn Seglem

When looking at literacy practices of youth, it is more likely to find teens interacting with new media or reading the latest titles written by young adult (YA) literature authors than voluntarily examining the themes and motifs of the classic literature most valued by school. At the same time, it is common to hear these very texts—highly valued by youth—dismissed as "brain candy" or vehicles of distraction rather than legitimate forms of literary activity. This contributes to educational policies that persist in privileging canonical fiction and nonfiction texts.

To counter this trend, this chapter demonstrates it is possible to critically engage in literary study with both new media and YA literature. By adapting traditional approaches to literary study to align with evolving, contemporary forms, teachers can provide youth with new lenses for viewing the texts they seem drawn to, and support their developing orientations toward being mindful producers and consumers of texts.

Traditional forms of literary study, such as close reading, reader response, and social semiotics, are evolving along with new media and youths' reading engagement practices. Drawn from professional development courses focused on YA literature, this chapter provides teachers, teacher educators, and education students examples of contemporary literary study of YA literature. It suggests that engaging in these newer forms of traditional literary study can bring teachers' practices up-to-date with ways youth are already exploring YA literature through new and evolving media.

EVOLVING DISCIPLINARY AND EDUCATIONAL PRACTICES

Typically, literacy educators can find themselves adopting one of four mindsets when considering media integration. Some educators—for myriad reasons—incorporate only traditional print texts like novels and essays into their instruction, leaving multimodal texts for students to discover on their own. Others take an opposite stance and completely abandon traditional print texts in efforts to maintain relevancy. Most contemporary language arts teachers, however, likely fall somewhere in the middle of these first two stances, respecting and adopting multimedia projects but ultimately privileging print texts by requiring multimedia texts to be accompanied by print texts in the form of commentary or reflection.

The examples shared in this chapter advocate for yet a fourth stance, a stance described by Leander (2009) as one where "the creations of meanings and effects upon audiences is of central concern, as are processes of production and interpretation that presume multimedia is not exceptional, but actually more typical than mono-media" (148).

Such a stance is necessitated by the evolving capacities and practices of new media. Considering the participatory ways of working and playing that have evolved with digital technologies, Jenkins, Kelley, Clinton, McWilliams, Pitts-Wiley, and Reilly (2013) suggest that society is at a critical juncture that "will redefine how knowledge is produced and stories shared for future generations" (11). Among other shifts, the interactive capabilities of new media are transforming the common ways author and audiences relate in the composition, interpretation, and analysis of literature.

Thomas and Stornaiuolo (2016), for instance, shared a range of ways that young people engage in new and social media to revise and otherwise restory their senses of self in the world and in relation to print and popular fiction, including restorying time and place, perspective, mode, identity, and the metanarratives of the literature they are consuming. They share, for instance, how young adults are using new media to recast popular depictions of the characters in YA literature with different racial make-up through creating and sharing images of "race-bent" characters.

As an example of another shift in literary engagement, in humanities, literary analysis is on the move with online mapping tools that are used to crowdsource fictional and historical on shared maps. These emerging forms of literary analysis add rhetorical, virtual, and spatial dimensions to traditional text-only literary analysis. Readers can use Google Earth to explore the regions where the YA literature they are reading are set, or create their own virtual landscape of the story on their own hometown using the GPS capabilities of a smartphone.

Forms of literary study have transformed and are transforming. The activities, genres, and expectations in education must likewise transform if teachers hope to stay up-to-date with the discipline's practices of literary study in a rapidly changing new media ecology (Smith and Kennett, 2017).

When approaching literacy instruction in this manner, a vital part of instruction rests in helping students learn to approach all texts—not just print texts—in a critical manner that questions whose interests are served in the production of texts (Gee and Hayes, 2011). All texts—whether they contain words, images, sounds, and a combination of these elements or engage interactive features—have an agenda, and language arts teachers are in a position to foster the practices needed to uncover that agenda.

YOUNG ADULT LITERARY ANALYSIS THROUGH NEW MEDIA MAKING WITH TEACHERS

As communication technologies evolve, and disciplinary practices of literary study transform with them, teachers need ongoing opportunities to familiarize themselves and engage with the tools, genres, and media that develop. This includes knowledge and use of modes, genres, and ways of interacting that are not typical in traditional schooling. Highlighted here are ways of engaging teachers as learners in the study of texts that often appeal most to youth: YA literature and new media, as well as how to analyze these texts in ways that mirror an evolving digital landscape.

The following examples are drawn from the authors' experiences of teaching courses focused on YA literature for both preservice and practicing teachers. These activities have been found to support critical and creative new media engagement in the evolving disciplinary practices of literary analysis. Through engaging in these activities with teachers, the aim was to provide the teachers with the approaches they can model for their own future students.

Rounds of *Close Reading* with YA Historical Fiction

With the English Language Arts Common Core State Standards has come a reemergence of an emphasis on "close reading." Like many new curricular initiatives, along with this emphasis has come a misunderstanding of close reading as a practice of rereading for discrete answers. To steer future language arts teachers away from this artificial rereading practice that frequents high school classrooms, Wiggins' (2013) approach to close reading can be emphasized. He suggests that to read a text closely, one must not only pay close attention to the facts and details contained within the page or on the screen, but also interpret those details through differing perspectives. This most often requires the reader to reread for different purposes.

Wiggins points to the seminal work *How to Read a Book* by Adler and Van Doren (1940) as one way to understand the different purposes for reading complex texts. He emphasizes four questions that readers must explore: What is the book about as a whole? What is being said in detail, and how? Is the book true, in whole or in part? What of it? The following is one way YA historical fiction has been paired with the use of various new media tools to help future teachers develop their own close reading practice with this approach. This example comes from a group of future teachers' close reading of the historical fiction *Code Talker* by Joseph Bruchac.

What is the book about as a whole? To help the future teachers begin to identify the themes and the author's development of themes, they were asked to develop a timeline of the events in *Code Talker* by Joseph Bruchac. Each group's approach to composing the timeline varied—some created timelines by hand, a low-tech version, while others utilized online interactive timeline applications.

When creating these timelines, they identified the events the author considered important and created a visual representation of how the author presented these events to readers. Then, the groups turned to the Internet as a source for a historically accurate timeline of the events depicted in the novel. By examining both timelines, they were supported in interpreting the theme of the book, in this case noting "the book focused more on the Navajos and the island hopping" in World War II.

What is being said in detail, and how? Next, teachers were asked to create a T-Chart that identified key events from the books on the left and inferences readers could make from these events on the right. This activity required them to return to events of the novel identified in their timelines and closely read the text in order to develop an understanding of the message the author was trying to convey—and importantly, it gave them a purpose for rereading the text.

They identified the data presented in the text: "August 6, 1945—Hiroshima is bombed with an atomic bomb and 70,000 people died. August 9, 1945—Nagasaki is bombed and 129,000 people died," and then interpreted the message the author intended to convey through the use of these data: "War is deadly and awful for everyone involved. Innocent people die and land is destroyed. Furthermore, the U.S. was kind of heartless by dropping the atomic bombs, because they caused so many innocent casualties."

Is the book true, in whole or in part? Once the teachers read through parts of the novel at least twice, they were asked to begin to interpret the events they had previously identified. They were prompted to return to the Internet and applications to determine the "truths" within the novel. Yes, they had compared dates, but the truth extends beyond numbers. To analyze truth within this telling of the Code Talkers, they located at least one primary document and one secondary source that would inform their understanding of the novel's depiction. In doing so, they explored the author's assertion that everything that happened to the novel's protagonist happened to the Navajos, breaking down their findings across texts in charts similar to table 7.1.

Creating this chart required the teachers pay close attention to the words within each text, highlighting the similarities they found and allowing them to identify the accuracy of the author's description of the events. Without almost instant access to primary and secondary sources via online collections, the teachers would have been hard-pressed to closely examine the effectiveness of the author's telling of (and his implicit argument about) *Navajo Code Talkers'* story.

What of it? Finally, once the teachers had completed each of the tasks associated with a different purpose for reading the text, they explored the book's significance by discussing questions designed to help them consider why the author felt the story was significant and whether or not the information in the book was important for them to know: Whose story is the novel portraying? What other stories were happening at the time? What choices did the author make when telling the story? How might the story have looked differently?

These questions, and others like them, prompted the teachers to think beyond surface meaning and summarization—too often, the version of close reading prevalent in secondary schools today. Rather, they considered how different aspects within the text and the author's craft contributed to the author's message.

The teachers' careful, repeated readings of the novel were enhanced by parallel close readings of online, multimodal, informational texts. Further, by engaging within small-group discussions, the future teachers deepened their understanding of the novel's message while developing the collaborative

Table 7.1. Chart comparing YA historical novel and primary and secondary source material

World War II: Navajo Code Talkers	*Navajo Code Talkers* and *The Unbreakable Code*	*Code Talker*
The first part, a 26-letter phonetic alphabet, used Navajo names for 18 animals or birds, plus the words ice for I, nut for N, quiver for Q, Ute for U, victor for V, cross for X, yucca for Y, and zinc for Z. The second part consisted of a 211-word English vocabulary and the Navajo equivalents.	The first letter of a Navajo word corresponded with one of the 26 letters in the English alphabet. Several different words were chosen to represent the more commonly used letters in order to make the code even more secure.	"For every letter of the English alphabet, a Navajo word was assigned." "So we added seventeen more Navajo words for A,E,I,O,U,D,H,L,N,R,S, and T" (pp. 77–78)

skills necessary for the participatory culture that permeates today's digital texts (Jenkins et al., 2013).

They continued to build their insights by engaging in the production rather than just the consumption of multimedia texts (Garcia, Seglem, and Share, 2013), synchronously composing a Google Slides presentation that merged hand-created images, primary source documents, and written words. In this instance, all of these elements were necessary to convey the message, emphasizing Leander's (2009) assertion that multimedia is the norm rather than the exception.

Reader Response to Critically Explore YA Literature about and "for" Youth

Like close reading, there are misconceptions about reader response. Rosenblatt (1990) emphasized that meaning is not just in the text, but rather, as the reader makes sense of a text, he or she is part of determining what a text means. Equally, she described this transaction as an exploration among not just the text and the reader but also, importantly, other readers and other texts. Pradl (1996) states: "Whether in harmony or dissonance, self-expression derives from a democratic procession of voices" (9). A "reader's response" is not an individual's siloed opinion, but rather, a transformation of meaning between texts, readers, and others.

As a pedagogical approach, Pradl (1996) further described reader response as "democratic teaching fosters multifaceted readings, and discussions are built on layers of agreement and disagreement. Literature education that promotes transformation always entails some significant change in perspective." With reader response in mind, reading and interpreting YA literature can be seen as an exploration of a "procession of voices." With the hope of having transformative moments, the following exploration with teachers was designed in such a way as to layer multiple perspectives together through rounds of multimodal dialogue.

In a course on literature and the adolescent experience, teachers focused on different groups of young people—like boys, Latinx, and LGBTQI—and the literature depicting and marketed to them. With a critical eye, teachers read YA literature for the stereotypes used and challenged in each piece. In a week focused on girls, for example, teachers chose a YA literature novel from a range of options, such as *Wintergirls* by Laurie Halse Anderson; *I Hadn't Meant to Tell You This* by Jacqueline Woodson; *Angus, Thongs and Full-Frontal Snogging* by Louise Rennison; and *Annie on My Mind* by Nancy Garden.

These novels were just the beginning of the "procession of voices" taken into consideration. The teachers looked at movie and book trailers, read articles from the news and from researchers about girls' reading practices, and surveyed social media for memes, GIFs, and videos that were surfacing about adolescent girls. They worked to reflexively read each of these texts, considering audience, intent, and evolving interpretations. From this, they crafted critical questions that would help in discussing how girls were depicted in YA literature and possible implications.

The week's focus culminated in a Socratic seminar centered around the questions that had surfaced, and the teachers engaged in close listening to peers' thoughts and representations of YA literature. To kick off each seminar, a group of teachers shared a new media composition that synthesized the various texts they had read, and raised the questions that remained. Figure 7.1 shares a representation of the multimedia compositions that were made, in this case a video, to introduce their questions for discussion.

The teachers' multimedia presentations typically included YA literature covers and quotes, memes about characters, clips from movies based on the YA literature they had read, and popular texts, like poems from spoken word poets that were being passed around among youth via social media in some of the schools where the teachers were teaching. The groups often shared that as they composed the video—layering images, quotes, and clips, with their questions—they felt their questions grow in importance.

The "procession of voices" did not stop there. Teachers turned their critical conversations into creative, multimodal dialogue. Using GDrive as a synchronous composing platform, teachers who read the same book collaboratively composed multimodal reviews in light of their layered conversations highlighting the perspectives developed through those exploratory experiences. A description of the Socratic seminar and their multimodal reviews were posted to a public blog, furthering the conversations and democratizing interpretations and readers' responses along the way (see http://developingwriters.org for links).

Exploring YA Literature's *Social Semiotics* through Hanging Out, Messing Around, and Geeking Out

Among the texts read and marketed to teens, transmedia storytelling, comics, and graphic novels stand apart with their uses of image, color, spatial arrangements, video, frames, sound, and symbols. They are also newcomer literary media for classroom study. When discussing these types of literary media with teachers, a social semiotics approach can help them focus on all that is happening in storytelling beyond words. They can consider the modes of communication used, the ways those modes are composed together, the resulting genres, and the discourse it is a part of producing (van Leeuwen, 2005).

Time	Video Screenshots	Voice Over
0:35	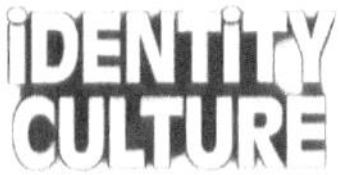iDENTiTY CULTURE	In considering 'identity' and 'culture,' we might ask: What does it mean to identify as an adolescent girl? How does culture shape adolescent girls' identity development?
0:38	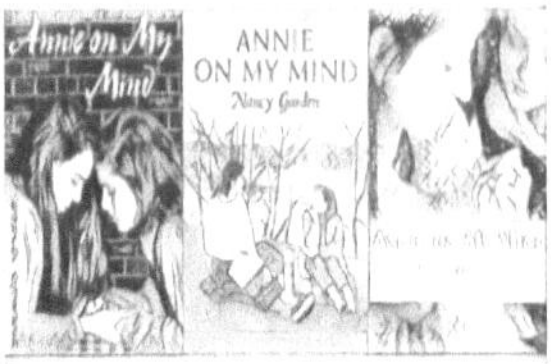Annie on My Mind ANNIE ON MY MIND Nancy Garden	Do the identities described in young adult literature parallel the girls' senses of self in the real world?
4:05	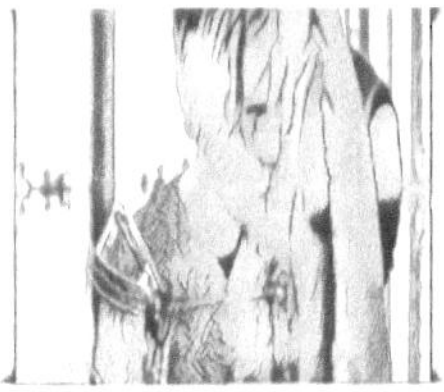	Most media marketed to young women has a main character whose issues revolve around a boy. Do you see any inherent problem in this?
4:20	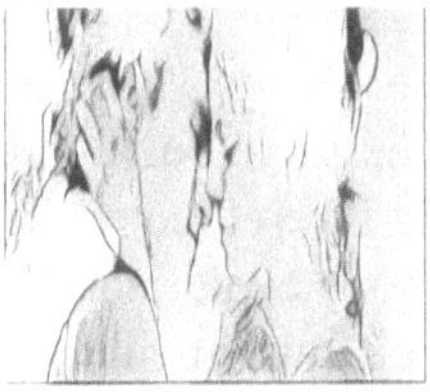	Why is it that so often a women's journeys in life, in texts, and on the screen pivot on their desire for the opposite sex?
4:28	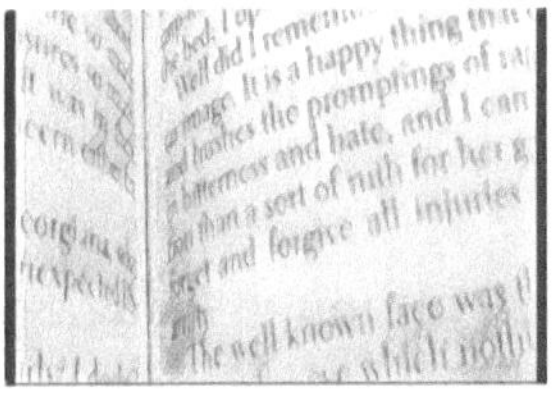	In the literature available to teens, is there any sign of breaking away from this axiom?
6:50	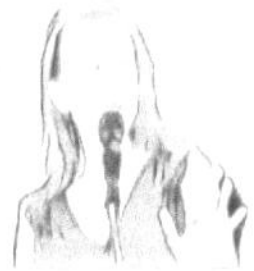	What if we took seriously the issues raised by Jeanann Verlee in her poem "To Adolescent Girls with Crooked Teeth and Pink Hair"?

Figure 7.1. Line drawings and text representative of screenshots and voice-over of a group's video prompt for a Socratic seminar

Teachers were invited to analyze literary media by not only reading in these forms but also trying their hand at composing with them. This can be done through the HoMaGo approach, which stands for Hanging Out, Messing Around, and Geeking Out. Mimi Ito and her colleagues (2010) developed this approach after watching how young people learn through digital media outside of school. HoMaGo is an approach well suited to a semiotic exploration of the types of literary media that have been traditionally outside the purview of schooling.

Teachers were first invited to *hang out* with transmedia stories, comics, and graphic novels. They followed the storylines and characters of transmedia such as *The Lizzie Bennet Diaries* across platforms including YouTube and Twitter to see how characters are presented through the modes and genres available in each space. They compared the differing visual and verbal stylings of comics creators and shared their favorites. They checked out online spaces, like Figment, Deviant Art, Goodreads, and FanFic.net, to see what modes of communication and genres of new media youth are using to engage in discussions about YA literature.

Then, it was time to *mess around* with YA literature through new media. After watching youth critique and celebrate texts in this new media, the teachers responded to the YA literature in kind. One group of teachers was particularly disconcerted with the depiction of adults as essentially uninvolved in the lives of teenagers in the YA literature they read. They found the "Y U no" meme, a humorous symbol well suited to expressing their growing frustration. In addition to messing around with the viral symbols in memes, teachers tried composing other types of literature responses, such as comics, video book trailers, and snap stories.

Finally, teachers were asked to *geek out* with one form of new media while they read a YA literature novel. This involved not just composing several literary responses using the medium of their choice but also employing what they learned from paying attention to the social semiotics of its use. In analyzing the semiotic interactions on Tumblr, one teacher noted the large number of fan-made images of quotations from books. She reflected in a public post:

> Through my exploration of Tumblr, I was shocked to find that a huge part of the Tumblr population were adolescents and that they included creative posts about books like *The Perks of Being a Wallflower* on their blogs. . . . It was interesting to see that there were a lot more of these visual representations that included actual text from the book than clips and snapshots from the screen adaptation.

In turn, she began to post her own visualizations of quotations, and reblogged the ones that moved her emotionally. She explained, "This somehow made my relationship with the book a bit more intimate and special. Had I just read the book and decided to only keep the text in mind and merely write out my analyses on a sheet of paper, I probably would not have been even close to artistically expressing my reactions to the book like I did on Tumblr." She was not alone. Many of the teachers discussed how moving from being primarily a consumer to also being a multimodal creator enhanced their engagement with their selected YA novels.

CONCLUSION

If teachers hope to keep pace with the ways young people are engaging with YA literature in a rapidly changing field of literary study, they, like their students, need opportunities to engage in multimodal interpretation and composition. With this in mind, this chapter highlighted re-envisioned versions of schooled approaches to close reading, reader response, and social semiotics with YA literature and new media.

Drawing from the ways youth are engaging with YA literature through new media, these activities focus on processes of production by layering varied approaches of multimedia exploration of YA literature together. When teachers or students weave multimedia texts with traditional texts, producing and interpreting texts simultaneously, they gain experience in making multimedia commonplace rather than exceptional. In doing so, language arts classroom practice can become more aligned with contemporary evolving types of literary study.

REFERENCES

Adler, M. J., and C. Van Doren. 1940. *How to Read a Book: The Classic Guide to Intelligent Reading*, revised edition. New York: Simon and Schuster.

Garcia, A., R. Seglem, and J. Share. 2013. "Transforming Teaching and Learning through Critical Media Literacy Pedagogy." *Learning Landscapes* 6 (2): 109–24.

Gee, J. P., and E. R. Hayes. 2011. *Language and Learning in the Digital Age*. New York: Routledge.

Ito, M. 2010. *Hanging Out, Messing Around, and Geeking Out: Kids Living and Learning with New Media*. Cambridge, MA: MIT Press.

Jenkins, H., W. Kelley, K. Clinton, J. McWilliams, R. Pitts-Wiley, and E. Reilly. 2013. *Reading in a Participatory Culture: Remixing "Moby Dick" in the English Classroom*. New York: Teachers College Press.

Leander, K. 2009. "Composing with Old and New Media: Toward a Parallel Pedagogy." In *Digital Literacies: Social Learning and Classroom Practices*, edited by V. Carrington and M. Robinson, 147–63. London: SAGE.

Pradl, G. 1996. *Literature for Democracy: Reading as a Social Act*. Portsmouth, NH: Boynton/Cook Publishers.

Rosenblatt, L. 1990. "Retrospect." In *Transactions with Literature: A Fifty-Year Perspective*, edited by E. J. Farrell and J. R. Squire, 97–107. Urbana, IL: National Council of Teachers of English.

Smith, A., and K. Kennett. 2017. "Multimodal Meaning: Discursive Dimensions of E-Learning." In *e-Learning Ecologies*, edited by B. Cope and M. Kalantzis. New York: Routledge.

Thomas, E. E., and A. Stornaiuolo. 2016. "Restorying the Self: Bending toward Textual Justice." *Harvard Educational Review* 86 (3): 313–38.

Van Leeuwen, T. 2005. *Introducing Social Semiotics*. New York: Routledge.

Wiggins, G. May 17, 2013. "On Close Reading, Part 2." [Web log comment]. https://grantwiggins.wordpress.com/2013/05/17/on-close-reading-part-2/.

Chapter 8

Seeing the World Differently: Remixing Young Adult Literature through Critical Lenses

Jennifer S. Dail and Aneté Vásquez

Students grow as tired of writing literary response papers as teachers grow of reading them. A stack of papers that rehashes the same themes and issues in stale ways brings no excitement or engagement to student learning. We live in a world that offers us much more opportunity to craft complex responses to how we are reading that world and moving through it, and it is our responsibility as teachers to help students engage in the world critically and respond to it authentically and meaningfully. Critical lenses help teachers facilitate such responses in students' interactions with texts, and young adult literature offers a safe platform for doing this.

Critical lenses invite students to deal with deep, often gritty, issues through highly approachable characters and narratives. Digital tools help students create authentic responses to these critical issues by allowing them to leverage visual elements and sounds to create robust responses that extend beyond text and print. By bringing these two theories into practice in a graduate teacher education course, we hoped to show students how to use digital media to engage themselves and their own students with other ELA concepts, such as literary response, specifically through a critical literacy lens.

PURPOSE OF THE STUDY

Henry Jenkins (2006) argues that schools have opportunities to engage students in a participatory culture in order to "develop the cultural competencies and social skills needed for full involvement" (4). Engaging students in participatory cultures taps into processes in which many of them already participate: affiliating in online communities (affiliations), producing new creative forms of text and media (expressions), working together in teams to complete tasks and develop new knowledge (collaborative problem solving), and shaping the flow of media (circulations).

Inspired and informed by Jenkins' work with students remixing *Moby Dick*, the authors of this chapter describe their work reading and remixing the novels *Tyrell* by Coe Booth (2007) and *Saint Iggy* by K. L. Going (2008) through the lens of critical literacy. The intent of this study is to examine and report on the following: How students adopt critical literacy lenses when analyzing literature and use remix as a concept in responding to literature, and how that employment of remix demonstrates processes described by Jenkins.

METHOD

Participants

The participants in this study are graduate students enrolled in a specialist degree program in secondary education at a large state university in a metropolitan area in the Southeast. The students currently teach English Language Arts in middle or high school settings and had been enrolled in a course titled Digital Media and Pedagogies in English Language Arts Education.

In this course, students explored current theoretical camps on teaching with digital media and examined practical means of applying those theories in their own classrooms. To that end, the course supported students in developing the technological skills required to develop multimodal products. Because the course is an upper-level graduate course, only nine students participated.

Exploring Critical Literacy

Literacy is often treated as an independent, neutral activity that addresses the ability to write and read. These discourses, though, disregard the fact that literacies are situated (Barton, Hamilton, and Ivanič, 2000), multiple (Garcia, Mirra, Morrell, Martinez, and Scorza, 2015), and interwoven with power relationships (Freire and Macedo, 1987). Critical literacy activities encourage readers to become active participants in the reading process and to interrogate texts at a deep level (McLaughlin and DeVoogd, 2004; Molden, 2007).

Students were introduced to the concept of critical literacy by reading and discussing Lewison, Flint, and Van Sluys' (2002) article "Taking on Critical Literacy: The Journey of Newcomers and Novices." In an online discussion board, students explained their understandings of critical literacy in their own words. Students were assigned to critical literacy groups, and their task was driven by both Daniels' (2002) literature circles and the four dimensions of critical literacy as described by Lewison et al. (2002).

Each student selected a role from among the first three dimensions from which to analyze the texts: disrupter of the commonplace, interrogator of multiple viewpoints, and investigator of sociopolitical issues. The final dimension required all group members to determine how they could take action for social justice with regard to the issues of inequity that emerged in the novels. The roles enabled students to problematize the issues in the novels and offered a structure for written journal responses as well as class discussions.

Journal responses were analyzed to determine if students could apply their knowledge of critical literacy in their analysis of the young adolescent novels. The information from the journals and discussions was used to reflect upon common threads dealing with critical literacy between the two novels and to create a multimodal remix to represent them.

Texts Selected

The novels *Tyrell* (2007) and *Saint Iggy* (2008) were selected because both texts, while introducing multiple issues to problematize, focus mainly on the issue of social class, a theme that "is present in many young adolescent literature novels, though the topic has not received extensive exploration from scholars" (Boyd and Pennell, 2015, 97). This is alarming considering that more than sixteen million children in the United States—22 percent of all children—live in families with incomes below the federal poverty level—$23,550 a year for a family of four.

Research indicates that poverty is the single greatest threat to children's well-being. Family poverty in the United States is typically depicted as a static, entrenched condition, characterized by large numbers of children, chronic unemployment, drugs, violence, and family turmoil (Wagmiller and Adelman, 2009). These are commonly held stereotypes about poverty we hoped to disrupt using the lens of critical literacy and the activity of remix. The selected works of adolescent literature facilitated reading from a resistant perspective.

The novel *Tyrell* (2007) addresses issues including incarceration, drugs, sexuality, gender roles, power, homelessness, racism, truancy, and social class. After fifteen-year-old Tyrell's father is imprisoned for dealing drugs in an attempt to earn money to pay rent and buy food, Tyrell, his younger brother Troy, and his mother lose their home and have to move into a grimy shelter in the Bronx provided for them by the New York City Emergency Assistance Unit.

Tyrell's mother is portrayed in a stereotypical way, as a woman who takes advantage of the system and has little desire to support her sons monetarily or emotionally. Tyrell attempts to fill this role. To earn money to move his family, he decides to throw a party in a deserted bus garage and charge admission. In addition to his financial problems, Tyrell is confused about his feelings for two girls, Novisha and Jasmine, and he is truant from school, which he considers useless.

Aside from the mother, the other characters are multidimensional and complex, like the world in which they live. There is an authenticity in the characters' language and life because the author, Coe Booth, was a consultant for the NYC Housing Authority and spent time with kids in circumstances similar to Tyrell's. The gritty setting of the Bronx illustrates the challenges teens living in poverty must surmount to survive. The authors selected this novel because it won the *Los Angeles Times* Book Prize for best young adult novel and because it provides an often underrepresented perspective.

Saint Iggy (2006) is the story of the title character, a sixteen-year-old on the verge of school expulsion. Iggy knows he needs a legal guardian and an attorney to represent him at the hearing where his fate will be decided. His parents, however, are habitual drug users, and his methamphetamine-addicted mother is missing. Living in public housing without a working phone to call his social worker, Iggy attempts to create a plan to contribute to the world.

Iggy turns to Mo, a pot-smoking, law school dropout, who is Iggy's mentor of sorts. While trying to create a plan for Iggy's hearing, Mo decides to buy drugs on credit from Freddie, the dealer Iggy blames for his parents' addiction. Author going juxtaposes Iggy and Mo, who is "renouncing" his wealthy upbringing, which Iggy gets to see when Mo takes Iggy to his mother's Upper East Side apartment to ask for money. The cultural divide between their upbringings is stark. Mo, however, must return to Freddie empty-handed, and Iggy is the one who becomes the mentor due to his knowledge of the neighborhood and its inhabitants.

Saint Iggy is a novel that confronts difficult subjects experienced by some young adults: broken families, poverty, drug addiction, lack of access to social services, and violence. It shows how these hardships have shaped the life of the protagonist and how hard Iggy must work to overcome them. We selected *Saint Iggy* because there are multiple parallels to *Tyrell*.

Texts and articles surrounding critical literacy have been highly theoretical. Only recently has critical literacy been put into praxis (Ives and Crandall, 2014; Morrell, 2015; Tracy, Menickelli, and Scales, 2016). In a review of literature on critical literacy, Behrman (2006) ascertained following six categories of practice: (1) reading supplementary texts, (2) reading multiple texts, (3) reading from a resistant perspective, (4) producing counter-texts, (5) conducting student-choice research projects, and (6) taking social action. This project enacted two of these categories: reading from a resistant perspective and producing counter-texts in the form of remix.

REMIX AS A RESPONSE TO CRITICAL LITERACY ISSUES IN THE TEXT

Preparing Students to Create Remixes

The act of remixing the text(s) as a literary response had two guiding instructional goals, which mirror those secondary teachers should implement in their own classrooms: help students compose and respond to film, video, graphic, photographic, audio, and multimedia texts and use current technology to enhance their own learning as appropriate in English education settings, and engage students in critical analyses of different media and communications technologies and their effect on students' learning in English education settings.

The description of the assignment learning activities leading up to the remix products was grounded in Jenkins' (2013) work on remix. Within that framework, remix may take any form, but must (1) remain recognizable as having the assigned work of literature as its source material, (2) alter/add to/advance the story substantially by transforming the literature, (3) take risk and push boundaries to present a creative product, (4) integrate multiple modes of composition, and (5) communicate the message clearly. Students wrote a two-part reflection of their composing process, including both the producer's and the reader's perspectives.

The steps of the project included a statement of intent, a detailed design plan, the final product, an examination of the product's impact, and a reflection on the process (Dail and Thompson, 2016). The early steps of a statement of intent and a design plan enable the teacher and peers to provide feedback early and throughout the composing process.

Students also submitted a draft of the multimodal remix for teacher and peer feedback. This process privileges traditional writing modes before moving into composing modes in order to support students in clearly articulating their thinking about the text prior to incorporating added elements that support and further illustrate that thinking.

Learning activities that applied theoretical readings on remix and multimodality (Dail and Thompson, 2016; Jenkins, 2006; Kress, 2003) also gave students time to tinker with putting the concept into praxis in a low-stakes environment while also receiving constructive feedback to apply in their creation of the final product. One of these activities asked students to examine teacher-offered examples of remix to determine and analyze the ways in which they did or did not met Jenkins' (2013) criteria for remix.

Another activity asked them to create their own remix by selecting any media (e.g., an image) and remediating it in some way that conveys meaning in a different way than the original media. They then had to explain why they are remediating the media in this way and what meaning they are applying to the media and what meaning it is still carrying, which leads to considering how those meanings work together or in tension with each other.

Students were given several examples of remix genres to consider for this learning activity, which informed the choices they made in their final product for the larger project. Examples included trading cards (e.g., Pokémon), posters, memes, making songs out of political speeches or poems, and digital poetry. This wide—and not all-encompassing—range of remix genres demonstrates the breadth of product possibility in asking students to take up this sort of work. Perhaps this ambiguity offers students the most freedom in composing while presenting a high level of uncertainty in the process and final product.

The Remix Products

Students' remixes varied in form to include character's social media accounts, character's letters, public service announcements (PSAs), and book trailers. Issie,[1] Greta, and Lily all teach in the same school and chose to create a book trailer for *Saint Iggy* for a classroom audience where students "are generally

Table 8.1. Overview of students' final remix products

Student	Type of remix	Positioning audience for independent thinking	Invoking sympathy or empathy for the characters	Taking up issues of race and gender	Representing missed, flat, or silenced voices	Examining the role of institutional systems
Sophie	Creating digital identities for characters		X	X	X	
Issie Greta Lily	Book trailer	X	X		X	X
Mitzie	Public service announcement	X	X			
Bert	Creating digital identities for characters	X		X		
Sadie	Diary from perspective of Tyrell's mother			X	X	
Ben	Letter to Tyrell from his father		X	X	X	
Tess	Book trailer	X			X	X

low-level, reluctant readers who don't pick up a book on their own." They continue to explain that these "students choose books by the cover and length rather than by the content of the back cover," and that they "have become so immersed in the visual images in their lives outside of school" that the trailer would have high appeal to them.

The students focused the trailer "on issues of disparity and wealth, dangers of drug culture, and the desperation felt by students in the current education[al] system, and the[ir] desire to contribute to society." Tess intended her students as the audience for her remix of *Saint Iggy*, stating that she wanted "them to gain interest in reading the novel because they may see themselves and the struggles of teenagers in the remix." Both of these remixes created an intentionally dark tone through gray or darker images and somber music; they linked this tone to the darkness of the issues explored in the book and in discussions framed by critical literacy.

Sophie's remix of *Tyrell* purposefully aimed to give Novisha, Ty's girlfriend, a voice by creating social media accounts for her on sites such as Instagram, Tumblr, and Facebook. She noted that she wanted readers to see Novisha as having "the potential to move beyond being defined by Tyrell," which led her to use the Instagram and Tumblr profiles to help Novisha communicate "her innermost thoughts through poetry, memes, and songs."

In contrast, though, Sophie used the Facebook profile as a more public face to mirror the second diary she kept for her parents. She reflected, "The reader may take different meanings from what is posted and may actually view Novisha as a confused teenager who does not know how to define herself, since her Facebook self conflicts with her Instagram and Tumblr self." Sophie recognized the tension she was deliberately creating between these profiles and how they contributed to further telling the narrative of the novel.

Analysis of the Remix Products

Since the students in the course were Educational Specialist (Ed.S.) candidates, we involved them with qualitatively analyzing the remix products for the actions they took and for the emotions they invoked by using open coding with descriptive data to support it. Students also had the opportunity to identify questions this cursory analysis raised for them as teacher researchers in a digital media environment.

Segments of data students coded for included positioning the audience for independent thinking; invoking sympathy or empathy for the characters; taking up issues of race and gender; representing missed, flat, or silenced voices; and examining the role of institutional systems. Students also analyzed the final remix products for their purpose and platform of production.

In analyzing products for the positioning of the audience for independent thinking, the effects of visual elements in relation to text became a focus.

Mitzie created a remix that focused on sharing facts about homelessness in response to *Saint Iggy*. Her remix was in the form of a video with images and facts about homelessness. She noted:

> I did not want to select heart wrenching or overly cliché pictures for fear of losing a broader audience base. The danger of creation lies in more possible attention being paid to the image and not to the startling fact presented in the caption—if one appeals more to the senses than the other, the audience will be torn by the visual and the text becomes lost. I searched for facts that would demand the reader think beyond the confines of the image and how the image could possibly be directly connected.

Issie, who created a book trailer, noted that her "remix will strive to introduce these themes in a manner that requires students to think about how these issues may affect them without explicitly 'preaching' at them." Tess noted of her remix, "I do not want the reader or viewer to feel guilt. I want to avoid the guilt that comes with letting your audience down. I want them to reflect and reposition themselves, if necessary."

Students' analyses and peer feedback indicated that where race issues were concerned, that Bert's remix addressed them most directly by juxtaposing a social media account for Tyrell with the account of a fictitious white adolescent male who had similar circumstances, friends, and problems but may be perceived and consequently addressed differently due to his race.

Students' reflections indicated that the combination of a specific reading lens with the multimodal response allowed them to focus on specific issues of their choice when creating a final analysis of the text. They did note that the examination of multiple perspectives is where most students focused their final remix. Based on our earlier discussion of critical literacy, this is not surprising because examining multiple perspectives is less intimidating for students in the early phases of grappling with these issues.

Student Observations about Remix

Even though the participants were graduate students, their concerns were no different than those often expressed by secondary students when engaging in this sort of work. They felt the time constraints when technology did not work as they anticipated or hoped. In these inevitable instances, the technology was felt more tedious than helpful. They also expressed concerns about whether or not their final product conveyed the intended message—a concern we would hope to see students exhibit with traditional literary essays as well.

The students also noted that the peer-review process helped them make adjustments with regard to their message both in content and in anticipated technology use. They also appreciated that the remix assignment allowed them to display their knowledge in a variety of ways, which they felt would be beneficial to their secondary students.

CONCLUSION

Students envisioned a variety of purposes for their remixes and defined their own audience and intent—something that is often absent in English Language Arts classrooms when traditional literary analysis essays are assigned. As might be expected, the digital products ranged in their degrees of sophistication; however, students fully engaged in the content. It is important to note that the sophistication of the final multimodal composition is far less important than students' understanding and application of the content—in this case the critical literacy themes in the novels.

Students used a variety of modes and skills in their multimodal remixes. Almost all students incorporated still images, and many combined those with video. Even the remixes that focused on social media sites integrated video and embedded links within their final product. The most common element across all of the products was the use of music. Of course, using these elements is not just about dropping them in to demonstrate dexterity with technology. It is about thinking critically about how visual, aural, and textual modes work together (or, in some cases, against each other) to create deeper meaning than what is achieved by text alone.

One of the strategies good readers use is making mental movies in their mind as they read (Elbow, 1998), and other strategies such as these allow students to compose and share those visual readings of text with others. As Bert noted in his reflection, remixing texts "shows that we make meaning through language, images, sounds, and color."

Students' reflections indicated that the combination of a specific reading lens with the multimodal response allowed them to focus on specific issues of their choice when creating a final analysis of the text. They felt that this presented more robust opportunities for expression than traditional response analysis essays.

NOTE

1. All student names are pseudonyms.

REFERENCES

Barton, D., M. Hamilton, and R. Ivanič, eds. 2000. *Situated Literacies: Reading and Writing in Context*. New York: Routledge.

Behrman, E. H. 2006. "Teaching about Language, Power, and Text: A Review of Classroom Practices That Support Critical Literacy." *Journal of Adolescent and Adult Literacy* 49 (6): 490–98.

Booth, C. 2007. *Tyrell*. New York: Push.

Boyd, A., and S. Pennell. 2015. "Batteries, Big Red, and Busses: Using Critical Theory to Read for Social Class in *Eleanor and Park*." *Study and Scrutiny: Research on Young Adult Literature* 1 (1): 95–124.

Dail, J. S., and N. Thompson. 2016. "Talking Back: Remix as a Tool to Help Students Exercise Authority When Making Meaning." *ALAN Review* 43 (3): 35–48.

Daniels, H. 2002. *Literature Circles: Voice and Choice in Book Clubs and Reading Groups*. Portland, ME: Stenhouse.

Elbow, P. 1998. *Writing without Teachers*. New York: Oxford University Press.

Freire, P., and D. Macedo. 1987. *Reading the Word and the World*. Westport, CT: Bergin and Garvey.

Garcia, A., N. Mirra, E. Morrell, A. Martinez, and D. Scorza. 2015. "The Council of Youth Research: Critical Literacy and Civic Agency in the Digital Age." *Reading and Writing Quarterly* 31 (2): 151–67.

Going, K. L. 2006. *Saint Iggy*. New York: Harcourt.

Ives, D., and C. Crandall. 2014. "Enacting a Critical Pedagogy of Popular Culture at the Intersection of Student Writing, Popular Culture, and Critical Literacy." In *Teaching towards Democracy with Postmodern and Popular Culture Texts*, edited by P. Paugh, T. Kress, and R. Lake, 201–20. Rotterdam, Netherlands: Sense Publishers.

Jenkins, H., October 19, 2006. "Confronting the Challenges of a Participatory Culture: Media and Education for the 21st Century." [Web log post.] http://henryjenkins.org/2006/10/confronting_the_challenges_of.html.

Jenkins, H., and W. Kelley. 2013. *Reading in a Participatory Culture: Remixing Moby Dick in the English Classroom*. New York: Teachers College Press.

Kress, G. 2003. *Literacy in the New Media Age*. New York: Routledge.

Lewison, M., A. S. Flint, and K. Van Sluys. 2002. "Taking on Critical Literacy: The Journey of Newcomers and Novices." *Language Arts* 79 (5): 382–92.

McLaughlin, M., and G. DeVoogd. 2004. "Critical Literacy as Comprehension: Expanding Reader Response." *Journal of Adolescent and Adult Literacy* 48 (1): 53–63.

Molden, K. 2007. "Critical Literacy, the Right Answer for the Reading Classroom: Strategies to Move beyond Comprehension for Reading Improvement." *Reading Improvement* 44 (1): 50–56.

Morrell, E. 2015. *Critical Literacy and Urban Youth: Pedagogies of Access, Dissent, and Liberation*. New York: Routledge.

Tracy, K. N., K. Menickelli, and R. Q. Scales. 2016. "Courageous Voices: Using Text Sets to Inspire Change." *Journal of Adolescent and Adult Literacy* 60 (5): 527–36. doi:10.1002/jaal.613.

Wagmiller, R. L., and R. M. Adelman. 2009. "Childhood and Intergenerational Poverty: The Long-Term Consequences of Growing Up Poor." New York: National Center for Children in Poverty. http://www.nccp.org/publications/pub_909.html.

Chapter 9

"Song of Myself": A Digital Unit of Study Remixed

Fawn Canady, Kymberly Martin, and Chyllis E. Scott

TELLING STORIES

Imagine sitting in front of a screen to view an assignment by Alejandro[1] (pseudonym), a tenth-grade student, posted publicly on Instagram, a social media photo app. He designed his Instagram to express something about his "essential self" for an assignment modeled after Whitman's celebrated poem, "Song of Myself." The images depict a sidewalk view of his route to school. There are no people in the images, simply concrete sidewalk, road, parking lots, and buildings. The captions, one or two sentences, tell the story of a Latino youth who must walk a line between external and internal expectations: peers, parents, teachers, society, and self.

The journey to success is fraught with assumptions. Alejandro writes, "Experts exclaim to me that in 30 years I will likely be in poverty." The last picture shows two heavy, metal doors opening to the school grounds. But it is not the end, he says: "All of this will be true unless I choose to reverse it." Now, read it backward, beginning with the last image and text. Read in reverse, the poem tells a fundamentally different story, a more optimistic one of a Latino boy resisting stereotypes: "I am truly intelligent . . . I can be successful."

To create his project, Alejandro capitalized on the functionality of Instagram (see Figures 9.1 and 9.2): viewers can scroll forward or backward through the images, experiencing a walk to and from school, with words that inverse meaning when read in reverse order. This innovative approach exemplifies just one of the multimodal creations from the Digital Self-Portrait project, the culminating experience of a unit of study designed to explore self-presentation through digital media and young adult literature (YAL). See Figures 9.1 and 9.2 for excerpts.

Figure 9.1. Alejandro's Instagram photo poem

Figure 9.2. Two heavy, metal doors opening to the school

The Digital Self-Portrait was a media representation of the "self." Students could choose any digital media (e.g., Instagram, Tumblr, Twitter, and YouTube) to compose a multimodal portrait. With *purposefully* vague guidelines, students gained freedom to remix modes and genres with which they were already familiar. The project consisted of a student-directed genre study (e.g., social media, digital video, and online comics), explorations of modes (e.g., text, images, and audio), peer workshops, and literature circles around YAL. YAL created an entry point into conversations about complex issues surrounding technology and identity.

Composing with multimedia transforms the classroom through networked technology, social learning, and a consideration of the affordances and constraints of various modes. In the Instagram example, the student looked at how he, as a Latino, is positioned by media and societal narratives. Instagram became a platform of resistance as he offered a counter-narrative to the societal account he often hears. Throughout this unit, students used their digital media savvy to probe socially embedded codes and explore identity. This is their story.

Problem: Seeing Teaching and Learning with Media Differently

This critical approach created a space for authentic use of media/technology in school-sanctioned classwork. It challenged assumptions surrounding teaching and learning with technology and digital literacies.

MISUNDERSTOOD: TEENS, TECH, AND YAL

Narratives about adolescents and technology smack of negativity. The tendency to blame technology for what is wrong in our classrooms stems from fears for "digital natives" (Prensky, 2001, 1), raised with twenty-four-hour advertising, information overload, and cyberbullying. While some of adults' concerns are founded, they often stem from a misreading of teens' engagement in and through media and technology. Teens participating in social media and networked spaces do what teens have always done: demonstrate resilience through creatively "repurposing technology to fulfill their desires and goals" (boyd, 2014, 212).

"Networked publics," as boyd (2014) describes, are *places* where young people try out identities by "imagining new possibilities, asserting control over their lives, and finding ways to be a part of public life" (boyd, 2014, 212). A more inclusive definition of literacies recognizes that people communicate and learn in multimodal ways. Teens are reinventing social contexts as well as out-of-school literacies, which educators can leverage to support in-school literacies.

YAL merges the out-of-school self with the in-school one. In YAL, students relate to familiar social issues like cyberbullying, gender mixing, and seeking connection. In class, students explore the representation of these issues, including how language influences perspective and affects behavior. For example, in *Guy in Real Life,* one of the gamers says to the protagonist:

> "We're not actually murdering a girl repeatedly. . . . Any rogue should be able to rez, vanish, sprint the hell out of here without my killing him again."
> "Her."
> "Him," he says. "This is not a girl, I promise. There are no girls on the internet."
> (Brezenoff, 2014, 146)

This dialogue brings up significant questions: What does it mean to be a "girl"? What is the difference between a girl in real life and one online? And what is the difference between "murdering" and "killing"? Plus, such texts raise important social questions like how does our virtual behavior affect us offline? In short, literature becomes another space to engage the students in conversations around technology and identities.

TEACHING DIGITAL COMPOSITION

A primary concern of teachers is how to prepare students for unpredictable futures and jobs. With technology's rapid evolution, schools are either not keeping pace with changes or are simply using technology as an add-on. How can we draw on the rich literacy practices of students' digital media use, interrogate how they perform identities in these spaces, and provide room enough to explore academic literacy without "schoolifying" it?

Insights gleaned from multimodal producers can inform classroom practices. Professionals do several activities in practice that teachers can do in the classroom: focus on the structures of various mediums, emphasize diverse sources of inspiration, discourage formulas or templates, encourage collaboration, and allow for nonlinear composing (Kist, 2014).

Challenges like access and infrastructure can arise at policy level, "Yet, we know that large-scale change is more likely to occur when classroom teachers lead the charge" (Hicks and Turner, 2013, 59). Additionally, professional organizations have underscored educators' responsibility to integrate new technologies (e.g., International Literacy Association and National Council of Teachers of English).

Still, multimodal composition and social media in the classroom present practical challenges for teachers, such as assessment. As instruction changes, assessment practices must also change "with and for digital writing" (Hicks,

2015, 2). To develop appropriate instructional practices, teachers can create standards-aligned assessments by closely examining student's work created with digital tools and media. Furthermore, they can examine how digital writing compares to traditional writing practices.

THEORETICAL FRAMEWORKS: CRITICAL LITERACY AND REMIX

New media has been characterized as democratizing because it encourages active participation and production of content. For this reason, the authors of this chapter use a critical literacy framework to examine youth engagement with technology and media. Critical literacy, at its most basic, is to examine something with a critical stance and to assume there is an underlying text. Critical stances examine power structures, especially those we take for granted as "just the way things are."

Working with adolescents to examine social codes is elemental to examining their relationship with technology. It fosters an understanding that signs and tools mediate learning and identity. Furthermore, critical literacy supports the concept that how we present ourselves for certain audiences is crucial to understanding social identity (Gee, 2000). People discern meaning in messages. Students can adapt preexisting social and cultural materials to remix them using a critical literacy lens.

Conversations around technology and adolescent use are particularly salient in the context of critical literacy, especially when adults misconstrue the ways in which youth interact. Furthermore, "Self-presentations are never constructed in a void" (boyd, 2014, 48). Adolescents actively create their identities through group affiliations (boyd, 2014). A critical analysis of YAL enables deeper reflection of the role of language in establishing relationships of power and allows students to transfer reflections to other contexts, such as their own group affiliations (Johnson, Mathis, and Short, 2016).

At heart, critical literacy allows readers to imagine alternatives, to move beyond the "what is" to the "what could be possible" (Johnson et al., 2016). Students become producers who remix existing narratives to generate new stories that both challenge the status quo and actively present possibilities for counter story.

Perhaps the real challenge for educators is to rethink teaching to reflect shifts in literacy without *colonizing* students' authentic, out-of-school use of digital media (Knobel and Kalman, 2016). Curriculum that reflects out-of-school connections and emphasizes learning as peer-driven, networked, and participatory motivates students to remix content knowledge in novel ways (Garcia, 2014).

Educators can look at how youth interact in networked spaces, remix semiotic repertoires, and participate in nonacademic cultures to reimagine what collaborative learning, affinities, and fluid mentorship might look like in the classroom (Jenkins et al., 2006). Remix culture emphasizes drawing on the ubiquitous resources available and, when combined with YAL, focuses on youth experiences and empowers students.

THE CONTEXT, TEACHERS, AND PROJECT

Kym Martin is an English teacher at a large, comprehensive public high school in the nation's fifth-largest school district. She is the second author of this piece. Kym's tenth-grade English Honors classes follow an Advanced Placement (AP) preparation curriculum. The school boasts an 81.9 percent score of three or higher on AP exams. Kym and her students have access to computer labs, but wireless Internet is not available to students. Blocks on social media websites also pose challenges.

Fawn Canady, a newly minted PhD, and Chyllis E. Scott, an assistant professor, were the three educators who worked together at various stages to design, implement, and assess the Digital Self-Project. The project was implemented during two school years (2015–2016 and 2016–2017). The study focused on student artifacts but did not include students' voice through interviews or observation.

Digital Self-Portrait Project

The Digital Self-Portrait asked students to examine the idea of an "essential self" and how this aspect of identity is portrayed through digital media. In order to do this, students participated in learning experiences such as literature groups with YAL that helped them examine their own media use and explore it from different perspectives. For the literature groups, students chose a YAL book that spoke to them from a predetermined list.

The YAL choices mirrored issues of technologically mediated identity. In *Fangirl*, the protagonist engages in fan-fiction in ways that challenge our concepts of originality, while *Random* and *Girl in Real Life* address relationships blurred by a false sense of distance, examining the very real consequences of online bullying and virtual roleplaying.** *Mr. Penumbra's 24-Hour Bookstore* explores our interdependence with (and overdependence on) new technologies. YAL presents issues that are salient to adolescents and reflect everyday choices about representation, interaction, and consequences. See Box 9.1 for book descriptions.

> **BOX 9.1. YOUNG ADULT LITERATURE DESCRIPTIONS**
>
> *Fangirl* is a good example of the alternate identities we adopt in different spaces and raises the question of remix and plagiarism: What is originality? The protagonist is cited for plagiarizing characters from her fan-fiction inspiration, which brings up the complicated issues of how we engage actively with texts and how we find and express an authentic voice.
>
> In *Guy in Real Life,* we follow characters who assume alternative identities in digital spaces and experience things from a different perspective. The boy in this book experiences complexities of being a female, including a stalking scene that brings the dangers of assumed and appropriated identities to the fore. The book offers an apt reminder that adolescence is a time where we try on different roles and how our media affinities identify us as certain "kind of people."
>
> In *Mr. Penumbra's 24-Hour Bookstore,* old technology meets new with a mystery like *The Da Vinci Code.* Where books are the ultimate of old technology, a staple in our lives and culture, gadgets and Google searches are our ever-present mediators. To solve the mystery of Mr. Penumbra's bookstore, old and new technology must team up. There are constant references to blogs, coding, typography, and an exploration of how overdependence on technology hinders a person's ability to function without it. Many have described the book as a love letter to books and to Google.
>
> *Random* is in one way a classic story about young people trying to fit in, but social media complicates it. Cyberbullying takes center stage in this text, as does the idea of being an upstander in digital spaces, creating and cultivating identities individually and in groups through social media, and really "seeing" people for who they are.

The YAL groups and learning opportunities built up to the Digital Self-Portrait Project, the unit's culminating project based on Whitman's celebrated "Song of Myself." The project asked students to extend Whitman's question of identity into a virtual world, in order to include factors like media consumption, time spent online, and sharing parts of life with an online audience.

In keeping with the guiding principle to allow students as much freedom as possible, the authors deliberately placed few limitations on the Digital Self-Portraits. The task: students share an aspect of their identity through a digital medium and include a form of writing to express their unique voice. The unit was structured in two phases: *Disconnect* and *Reconnect*.

DISCONNECT PHASE

In the Disconnect phase, students began with the Note to Self "Infomagical" podcast, a week of daily challenges designed to cut through information overload. Each challenge presented expert advice around de-cluttering tech-rich lifestyles. After participating, students noted one thing that stood out for them from the day's challenge, predominantly citing "awareness" as the big takeaway.

The takeaways reflected what students found relevant in the podcast. Some students noted that they needed to be more mindful of their media use and the way they socialize online. Other takeaways included the myth of multi-tasking, being more present, and not to "waste time" in "mindless" pursuits. Students considered very specific points, such as "It takes 7 minutes to start a real conversation" and "I learned that people take more interest in talking to strangers."

Throughout the unit, students read technology-related YAL and engaged in literature circles or, in the second iteration, an online book club. The online Book Club was a virtual space for critical discussions in Edmodo, an educational social media site that resembles Facebook. Modeled after literature circles but less structured, the Book Club helped students identify motifs across learning experiences.

Students analyzed the thematic and rhetorical choices of the author and talked about how his/her choices convey purpose and voice. Furthermore, the networked discussions between students and teacher mirrored participatory communities in the digital sphere: low barriers of participation, fluid exchange of ideas, and non-hierarchical learning (Jenkins et al., 2006).

Some students loved the online discussions for their simplicity and ease: "The computer aspect of it being online made it easier on my part. It was a good facilitator of knowledge and was a lot less stressful than a seminar. Also, it gave us tangible feedback from peers." Others disliked it because it felt impersonal: "I slightly hated posting my responses online. I felt like no one was really reading them. And that no one really cared about what I had to say." Though not all students shared an affinity toward the online discussions, the process did stimulate valuable conversations about communication in a digital space.

Throughout the unit, Walt Whitman's "Song of Myself" served as an anchor text, with particular focus on Canto 4 (Box 9.2). Whitman's cataloguing parallels the frenetic pace of information overload, one of the opening topics of the Disconnect phase. Students identified with the overwhelming amounts of people, places, and emotions seemingly piled on top of each other. Still, Whitman experiences ecstatic engagement with his world, as well as an essential self-separate from it all: "They are not the Me myself" (Whitman, 1881, 32).

Students responded to the duality Whitman established and shared their own experiences with the multitudinous feelings and responsibilities that "come to [them] days and nights and go from [them] again" but do not define their essential self. To further the reflective process, students wrote an imitation poem following Whitman's format by replacing the details of his everyday life with their own. The imitation poem helped them consider who and what they identify with and gave them a template for exploring their own voice through writing.

BOX 9.2. "SONG OF MYSELF" (1892 VERSION)

By Walt Whitman

4
Trippers and askers surround me,
People I meet, the effect upon me of my early life or the ward and city I live in, or the nation,
The latest dates, discoveries, inventions, societies, authors old and new,
My dinner, dress, associates, looks, compliments, dues,
The real or fancied indifference of some man or woman I love,
The sickness of one of my folks or of myself, or ill-doing or loss or lack of money, or depressions or exaltations,
Battles, the horrors of fratricidal war, the fever of doubtful news, the fitful events;
These come to me days and nights and go from me again,
But they are not the Me myself.
Apart from the pulling and hauling stands what I am,
Stands amused, complacent, compassionating, idle, unitary,
Looks down, is erect, or bends an arm on an impalpable certain rest,
Looking with side-curved head curious what will come next,
Both in and out of the game and watching and wondering at it.
Backward I see in my own days where I sweated through fog with linguists and contenders,
I have no mockings or arguments, I witness and wait.

The YAL was integrated in subtle ways. For example, one student imitated Whitman's poem in Box 9.3. The following lines are also echoed in the novel *Fangirl*:

> My homework, fandoms, attire, manner, games, worries,
>   The total unimportance of a crush on a fictional character.

This is another example of how YAL relates directly to the lived identities of students.

Another student, Amanda, drew on themes of cyberbullying echoed in *Random*. She viewed herself as adopting an outsider's perspective, because

---

BOX 9.3. "SONG OF MYSELF" IMITATION POEM

Whippersnappers and tricksters surround me,
People I meet, the effect upon me back in the day or the present and future, or in another dimension
The current events, memes, celebrity gossip, the latest trend, the shows that you have to binge watch over a weekend,
My homework, fandoms, attire, manners, games, worries,
The total unimportance of a crush on a fictional character,
The travels, or sickness of friends and family or getting a job or being cool or getting my learner's permit or deciding what classes I want to take or what to do after I graduate
Everyday struggles, the failure looms, the judgment is inescapable, the procrastination is (I'll get back to this later),
These come to me days and nights and go from me again,
But they are not the Me myself
Apart from the crowd stands what I am,
Stands taciturn, resolute, nutty as a fruitcake, quirky, unruffled,
Looks low-key, is eager, or apprehensive, on what's to come on the Highway to Hell (AC/DC)
Both in and out of the game and watching and wondering at it.
Backward I see in my own days where I stood my ground, my head in the clouds,
I have no complaints or regrets, I simply listen and anticipate.
I believe in you my soul, that you will lead me along the right path towards my future, wherever I go. So, my soul let us cruise the Seven Seas as pirates, searching for the meaning of life.

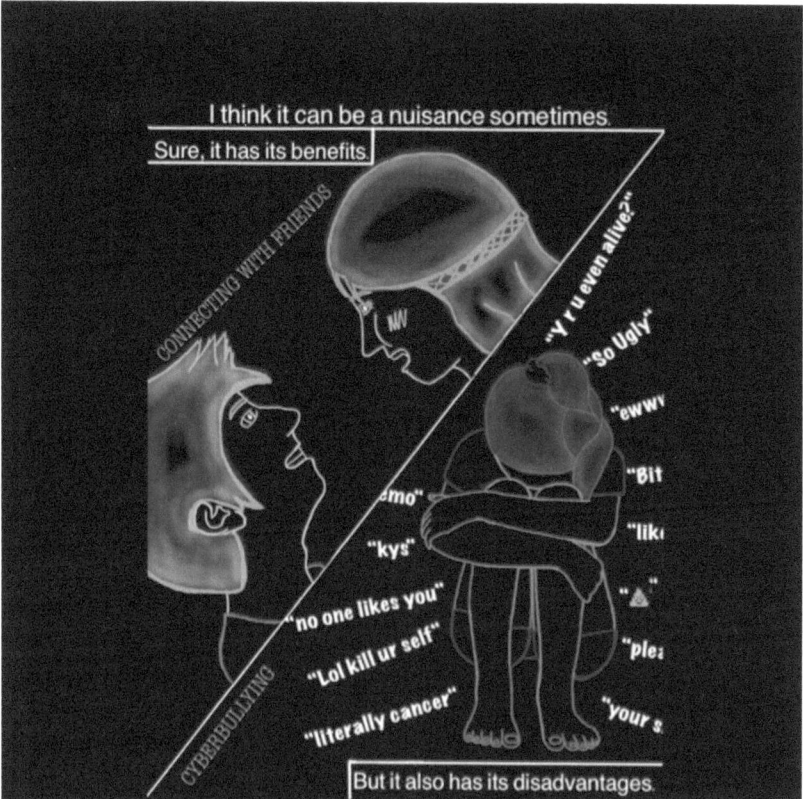

Figure 9.3. Amanda's digital comic "Offline"

she did not have a phone or access to social media. In her hand-drawn digital comic, "Offline" (shown in Figure 9.3), Amanda explored the positives and pitfalls of an "always on" life. Whether or not the inclusion of motifs from the books was intentional, the authors knew that students could discuss them.

RECONNECT PHASE

Next, in the Reconnect phase, students explored how to use media more deliberately to communicate with others. Students became aware of the choices they already make about purpose and audience through social media. The teacher introduced a variety of texts and multimedia to help students think through the ways in which meaning is constructed. Explicit teaching about digital media compositions is often a part of classroom experiences, but the teacher wanted to encourage a critical approach by beginning with students' responses and then coconstruct meaning together through a mentorship or facilitator model.

Fawn and Kym introduced visual rhetoric through a series of well-known images. They discussed composition and mythology (Barthes, 1957) to reveal how images serve as powerful forms of direct and indirect communication. These images included Dorothea Lange's "Migrant Mother," the iconic *Time* and *Newsweek* covers of O. J. Simpson, and screenshots of Kylie Jenner's Instagram. Clips of Taylor Swift's "Wildest Dreams" and Beyoncé's "Formation" music videos were shown to explore how people can use an image's unstated mythology to reinforce or subvert cultural assumptions.

Conversations around visual rhetoric were paired with an excerpt from Peggy Orenstein's book *Girls & Sex* (2016) to explore how social media changes our behavior from "amp[ing] up . . . self consciousness" to "talking about the self as a brand rather than something to be developed within" (18). Themes in popular media were mirrored in the YAL books. In the end, students viewed self-presentation with a fresh perspective through critical reading.

ASSESSING A PROJECT WITH NO PARAMETERS

To prepare the unit, the team identified all Common Core State Standards that applied to the instruction, then honed in on the specific standards to teach and assess. The authors focused on writing standards (like W.9–10.3D) that develop students' voice with precise words, telling details, and sensory language; and standards that require the use of digital media (SL.9–10.2, SL.9–10.5, and W.9–10.6) publish shared writing products (Canady, 2017).

Because of the Digital Self-Portrait's broad parameters, the teacher and researchers understood that no single rubric, no matter how detailed, could fit all projects, so they placed responsibility on the students to identify their own individual terms for evaluation, using a contract template to help them think through their choices, which can be found in appendices A and B (Canady, 2017).

Assessing multimedia projects can be stressful because teachers often feel they must be "experts" before they can begin to design instruction. Inviting students to identify the specific terms of their assessment means that even those teachers who are least comfortable with technology can still incorporate multimedia projects in their classrooms. Rather than manipulating the online medium to fit a more traditional academic structure, the authors wanted students to use media the way it was intended, thereby offering a better understanding of communication within each platform's affordances and constraints (Hicks and Turner, 2013).

Students drew up their evaluation contracts four weeks into the unit, after ample time exploring and analyzing digital samples. After students wrote and submitted a contract draft, each student had a one-on-one conference with the teacher to review his or her project and the terms of his or her contract (see Box 9.4). Together, teacher and student discussed ways to make the terms more specific.

BOX 9.4. STUDENT SAMPLE DIGITAL SELF-PORTRAIT CONTRACT

In order to get an A on my Digital Self-Portrait, I will . . .

- Post a working link to my project on Edmodo no later than 8 am on 5/18.

Writing:

- I will include at least 300 words in my writing.
- My writing will reflect my theme of Self-Discovery and Connection.
- My writing will be free of mechanical errors.
- My writing will include stylistic features like metaphors, similes, sensory details, and strong word choice.
- The content of my writing will be reflective by sharing things that make me happy and sharing my passions, interests, hobbies, and important people.

Creativity and Effort:

- I will show creativity by arranging my photos in a new and unique way, including colorful images, applying unique filters to my photos to make certain ones stand out, including a variety of stylistic features in my writing, using unique quotes that reflect complex ways of thinking, taking a new spin on an old idea, and including multiple elements of self.
- I will demonstrate effort by having a minimum of thirty photos, taking my writing through multiple revisions, connecting all photos and writing to my theme, and having clean images and illustrations without errors.

> ***Presentation:***
> - Poise
> - Voice
> - Life
> - Eye contact
> - Gestures
> - Speed
>
> By signing below, both parties agree to the aforementioned terms. The student will receive an A on his/her Digital Self-Portrait by meeting the above guidelines in their entirety.
>
> Date: Student Name: Student Signature:

Students' revisions reflected the teacher's guidance. One student who planned to use Instagram for his project initially wrote, "I will include many pictures" as a way to show his effort, which he later revised to, "I will post 18 pictures that I have personally taken of the skateboarding lifestyle." To express creativity, a student writing a music blog initially said she would use "unique stylistic features in her writing," which she later revised to, "I will include imagery, metaphors, and strong verbs to convey how music affects me." The process of student-driven evaluation engaged students in the meta-cognitive process, resulting in deliberate choices.

THE FINAL DIGITAL SELF-PORTRAIT PROJECT

Despite uncertainty about how students would react and whether the quality of their products would merit such an extensive unit, the final projects turned out to be far more innovative and inspiring than anticipated. Of the digital mediums, Instagram was the crowd favorite. The majority of students used it for their final projects. Though some used the platform in predictable ways (to display pets, friends, and family), others transformed its intended use to create something fresh and meaningful, like Alejandro, who opened the chapter.

Alejandro's project used a ubiquitous social medium to examine positions of power and privilege connected to his place within a preestablished social hierarchy. On one reading, his role is passive with cultural assumptions predetermining his fate; on the reverse reading, Alejandro actively challenges these assumptions and provides a counter-narrative of his success.

Alternatively, another student's Instagram project revealed the collaborative, participatory nature of digital literacy when she asked friends and strangers on Facebook, ranging in ages from ten to seventy-eight, to take pictures of their hands and respond to questions about their joys and regrets. She then posted participants' pictures on Instagram and included their responses in the captions. Another student displayed multimodal aspects of social media by creating Vines[2] of her small pleasures, using Instagram to display the Vines, and then writing poems in the captions about each one.

Students used other digital mediums beyond Instagram in similarly inspiring and creative ways, such as a YouTube video asking, "Why are we all so different? Why is the world so beautiful?" One student read and animated her Whitman imitation poem; others created Draw-My-Life videos to capture personal history, time-lapses of their artistic endeavors, and short documentaries about life philosophies.

Students constructed video games, blogs, and Pinterest boards. One student looked at her digital identity as a reader by writing reviews of her favorite books on Goodreads. Her project aligned closely with an academic identity that was influenced by her outside reading of YAL:

> I'm fairly new to the reading scene. I only started to really read books in January 2013, starting with (*cringe*) the Divergent series, moving on to Rainbow Rowell's books. Now, I read everything, close to 80 books a year which is absolutely ridiculous now that I think about it right now. That's almost two books a week . . . myself being my only guide as I was the only one out of all my friends who read this much in middle school.

Repeated references to her own readers (audience) reveal how she took her reader identity to a level that extends beyond school and allows her to participate in communities aligned with her affinities. The freshness, energy, and creativity of students' projects, as well as their honest reflections as consumers and producers of digital technology, are evidence that teachers do not have to put digital literacies *before* critical literacies (Pandya and Avila, 2014). Students can achieve awareness and growth through multimodal composition.

YAL, Media, and New Perspectives

In the time it took to write this piece, the media students used has likely shifted. Instead of focusing on the technology, then, the authors encourage a deeper look at students' relationships with technology, through technology, and how this technology influences the locus of self, particularly through communication.

The key to a critical approach was to create space for authentic use of media/technology in school-sanctioned classwork. The Digital Self-Portrait's authenticity afforded an examination of people's intimacy with technology gadgets and the Internet during the most mundane and dramatic parts of life, not just time spent at school.

The project also opened the question of how each of us fits into a broader, ongoing conversation. Reading YAL provided a variety of critical perspectives that allowed these students the chance to explore themes in various contexts. As researchers and teachers, the Digital Self-Portrait project demanded that the authors closely examine their own assumptions about technology and teens, and, in the likeness of this digital world, we both fear and love, to participate in new and exploratory ways.

CONCLUSION

Students are using digital media, though they may not be conscious of *how* they are using semiotic resources to communicate. The Digital Self-Portrait was open ended, inviting students to explore media and self-presentation in a critical way. Kym, the teacher, admitted that the process was often messy and uncomfortable. However, she understood on a fundamental level that she had to muster the courage to give the reins over to her students. One student, tenth-grader Darrin, intuitively understood this concept when he wrote in his Instagram portrait, "Although the digital self-portrait was only assigned this quarter, in reality I have been doing this project ever since I was first introduced to social media."

NOTES

1. Pseudonyms have been used for all students to protect anonymity.
2. Vines are digital videos typically 6½ seconds long that run in continuous loops.

REFERENCES

Barthes, R. 1957. *Mythologies*. New York: Hill & Wang.
Beyoncé. December 9, 2016. *Formation*. https://www.youtube.com/watch?v=WDZJPJV__bQ.
boyd, d. 2014. *It's Complicated: The Social Lives of Networked Teens*. New Haven, CT: Yale University Press.

Brezenoff, S. 2014. *Guy in Real Life*. New York: HarperCollins.
Canady, F. E. 2017. *"Already Writers": A Case Study in Assessment and Visual Rhetoric Connections in Digital Multimodal Composition* (Unpublished doctoral dissertation). University of Nevada, Las Vegas.
Garcia, A., ed. 2014. *Teaching in the Connected Learning Classroom*. Irvine, CA: Digital Media and Learning Research Hub.
Gee, J. P. 2000. "The New Literacy Studies: From 'Socially Situated' to the Work of the Social." In *Situated Literacies: Reading and Writing in Context*, edited by D. Barton, M. Hamilton, and R. Ivanic, 180–96. London: Routledge.
Hicks, T. 2015. *Assessing Students' Digital Writing: Protocols for Looking Closely*. New York: Teachers College Press.
Hicks, T., and K. Turner. 2013. "No Longer a Luxury: Digital Literacy Can't Wait." *English Journal* 6: 58–65.
Jenkins, H., K. Clinton, R. Purushotma, A. J. Robison, and M. Weigel. 2006. *Confronting the Challenges of Participatory Culture: Media Education for the 21st Century. An Occasional Paper on Digital Media and Learning*, edited by John D. and Catherine T. MacArthur Foundation. Cambridge, MA: MIT Press.
Johnson, H., J. Mathis, and K. Short. 2016. "Connecting Critical Content Analysis to Critical Reading in Classrooms." In *Reframing Perspective: Critical Content Analysis of Children's and Young Adult Literature*, edited by H. Johnson, J. Mathis, and K. Short, 185–99. New York: Routledge.
Kist, W. 2014. "The Writing Process and Multimodal Composition: Conversations with Four Artists." In *Exploring Multimodal Composition and Digital Writing*, edited by R. E. Ferdig and K. E. Pytash, 68–83. Hershey, PA: IGI Global.
Knobel, M., and J. Kalman, eds. 2016. *New Literacies and Teacher Learning: Professional Development and the Digital Turn* (1–20). New Literacies and Digital Epistemologies Series (Book 74). Bern, Switzerland: Peter Lang, Inc.
Lange, D. 1936. *Migrant Mother*. Photograph. Library of Congress. http://www.loc.gov/rr/print/list/128_migm.html.
Levine, T. 2014. *Random*. New York: Simon Pulse.
New York Public Radio, producer. 2016. *Note to Self: Infomagical* [Audio podcast]. https://project.wnyc.org/infomagical/.
Orenstein, P. 2016. *Girls & Sex: Navigating the Complicated New Landscape*. New York: HarperCollins.
Palmer, E. 2014. *Teaching the Core Skills of Listening and Speaking*. Alexandria, VA: ASCD.
Pandya, J. Z., and J. Avila, eds. 2014. *Moving Critical Literacies Forward: A New Look at Praxis across Contexts*. New York: Routledge.
Prensky, M. 2001. "Digital Natives, Digital Immigrants, Part 1." *On the Horizon* 9 (5): 1–6.
Rowell, R. 2013. *Fangirl*. New York: St. Martin's Griffin.
Sloan, R. 2012. *Mr. Penumbra's 24-Hour Bookstore*. New York: Picador.
Swift, T. August 30, 2015. *Wildest Dreams* [Video file]. https://www.youtube.com/watch?v=IdneKLhsWOQ.
Whitman, W. 1881. *Leaves of Grass*. Philadelphia: Rees Welsh & Co.

Appendix A

IDEAS FOR DIGITAL SELF-PORTRAIT CONTRACT TERMS

In order to get an A on my Digital Self-Portrait I will . . .

- Post a working link to my project on Edmodo no later than 8am on 5/18

Writing:

- I will include _____ amount of writing (number of posts, length of writing, word count, etc.)
- My writing will be free of mechanical errors.
- My writing will reflect my theme of _____
- My writing will include stylistic features like _____, _____, _____, and _____ (include as many as you like)
- The content of my writing will be reflective by. . . (sharing my passions/interests/hobbies/important people/mistakes/areas of growth/desires & dreams/things that make me happy; telling stories about important experiences; revealing aspects of my life that no one knows; allowing myself to be vulnerable in the content I share, etc.)

_____ points

120   *Appendix A*

Creativity:

- I will show creativity by _____ (ideas might include: arranging my photos to parallel a unique vision, including colorful images, applying unique filters to my photos to reflect my mood, layout, illustrating my images, connecting my images and writing in meaningful ways, including a variety of stylistic features in my writing, choosing unique quotes that reflect complex ways of thinking, making my own pins, adding humor, adding transitions and effects to the editing, writing my own script/song/poetry, taking a new spin on an old idea, including multiple elements of self, etc.)

    _____ points

Effort:

- I will demonstrate effort by _____ (ideas might include: ensuring clear recordings/videos that are free of background noises or distracting sounds, the number of pictures or length of writing, the amount of filming & editing, customizing my blog/website to be aesthetically pleasing through colors/images/fonts/structure, taking my writing through multiple revisions, connecting all photos/writing/fonts/colors to my theme, length of video, clean images/illustrations/videos with no errors, taking all the pictures myself, including at least XX number of posts/images/captions, learning XYZ program to create a video game, etc.)

    _____ points

Presentation:

- Poise
- Voice
- Life
- Eye Contact
- Gestures
- Speed

    _____ points

    TOTAL = _____ (how many points should this project be worth?)

By signing below, both parties agree to the aforementioned terms. The student will receive an A on his/her Digital Self-Portrait by meeting the above guidelines in their entirety.

| Student Name | Student Signature | Date |

| Teacher Name | Date |

REFERENCE

Palmer, E. 2014. *Teaching the Core Skills of Listening and Speaking*. Alexandria, VA: ASCD.

Appendix B

DIGITAL SELF-PORTRAIT: STUDENT REFLECTION

1. What elements of your Digital Self-Portrait were you particularly proud of and why?

2. Knowing what you do now, what, if anything, would you do differently? Explain.

3. If a stranger saw your Digital Self-Portrait on the Internet, would they get a good sense of who you are? Explain your reasoning.

4. With which medium did you choose to communicate something about yourself? Do you feel that this was an adequate method for communicating your theme? Explain.

5. Based on the criteria you developed for your Digital Self-Portrait, what grade do you deserve for the project and why? (Please give specific reasons/evidence.)

Index

academic life, 41–42
Adler, M. J., 81–82
adolescence: on civic engagement, 42; literacy practice of, 2; on social codes, 105
ALAN. *See* Assembly on Literature for Adolescents
All American Boys (Reynolds and Kiely), 32, *35–36*; collaboration on, 12; in digital environment, 9–16; discussion on, 34
Alvermann, D., 2
Anderson, M. T., 70
annotation, 13–14
anticipation guide, 23
Appleman, D., 30
apps, 72
Assembly on Literature for Adolescents (ALAN), 66
authentic engagement, 35
avatars, 13

Bardugo, L., 22
Benincasa, S., 53
Bergmann, J., 19, 20–21, 24
Blackboard Collaborative, 68–69
#BlackLivesMatter, 45
blogging, 69
Blume, Judy, 2

book activities, 82–83
book club, 108
The Book Thief (Zusak), 28–29
book trailers, 12, 98
Booth, Coe, 92–94
boyd, d., 103–104
Brickey, Kristine, 47–48
Brookfield, S. D., 32
Bruchac, Joseph, 82
buzzing, 32–33
By Any Media Necessary: The New Youth Activism (Jenkins, Sangita, Gamber-Thompson, Kligler-Vilenchik, and Zimmerman), 42

Canady, F. E., 106
circulation, 42, 49
civic engagement: adolescence on, 42; agency and, 43; need for, 42–43; teachers on, 46; through YAL, 41–52
classroom pedagogy, 28–29
classrooms: contemporary English, 43; of ELA, 44, 99; of Glose, 11–12; standards for, 2–3; students in, 1–6; virtual education in, 73–74; virtual students in, 71; YAL in, 64. *See also* virtual classrooms

Click Here (To Find Out How I Survived the Seventh Grade) (Vega), 69
Code Talker (Bruchac), 82–83
collaboration: on *All American Boys*, 12; students on, 56, 60–61, 69, 71–72
Common Core State Standards, 54, 112
communication, 2
consumption, 54
context, 29–31, 106–108
conversational learning, 28
Copeland, M., 32–34
critical dialogues, 43–45
critical lenses, 91–92
critical literacy: digital literacies and, 115; exploring of, 92–93; readers on, 105–106; remixes with, 105–106; teachers on, 73; technology in, 105; texts on, 94; youth on, 105
critical readers, 28; students as, 43; of YAL, 31–32
critical reading, 28, 31–32, 43, 112
curriculum, 4, 60, 64, 105

dialogues, 42, 44–46, 67. *See also* critical dialogues
digital:
 citizen, 3, 45;
 comic, *111*;
 composition, 104–105;
 devices, 9–10;
 discussion board, 33–34;
 environments, 4, 9–16;
 literacies, 60–61, 103, 115;
 media, 4, 41, 42, 101, 105, 116;
 reading, 10–11, 16;
 samples, 113;
 self-portrait contract, *113–14*, 114–15;
 spaces, *107*;
 tools, 4, 5, 10, 91, 105;
 video, 20;
 work, 3, 5–6
Digital Self-Portrait project, 101, 103, 106, 107, 112, 114–16

disciplinary practices, 79–81
disconnect phase, 108–109
discussions: on *All American Boys*, 34; answers in, 27; on *The Book Thief*, 28; on media, 30; rubric for, 33–34; in Socratic Circles, 31, 34; students on, 108; teachers on, 29; on YAL, 73

English Language Arts (ELA): access points in, 48; classrooms of, 43–48, 99; critical dialogues in, 43–44; YAL and, 41

Facebook, 68, 97
Feed (Anderson), 70
Fitzgerald, F. Scott, 53–61
Fleischman, Paul, 46–47
Flint, A. S., 92–93
flipped learning, 19–24
Forever (Blume), 2
formative assessment, 58–59

Gamber-Thompson, N., 42
gaming, 53–61
Girls & Sex (Orenstein), 112
The Girl Who Was on Fire: Your Favorite Authors on Suzanne Collins' Hunger Games Trilogy, 30
global collaborator, 3
Glose: classrooms of, 11–12; functionality of, 11; multimodal affordances of, 14–15; readers within, 11–15; teachers on, 11–12, 15–16
Going, K. L., 92–94, 98
Google Hangouts, 11, 12, 14
Google Slides, 84
Great (Benincasa), 53
The Great Gatsby (Fitzgerald), 53–61, *59*

Hawisher, G. E., 3–4
Hicks, T., 48
historical fiction, 81–82, *83*

How to Read a Book (Adler and Van Doren), 81–82
Humans of New York, 46

ideas, 31–34, 71–72
identities, 12–15
inner circle, 31
Instagram, 101, *102*, 114–15
interaction, 65
investigation, 42, 46–47
Ito, Mimi, 87

Jake Reinvented (Korman), 53
Jay Gatsby mansion, *59*
Jenkins, H., 42, 91–92, 95
journal responses, 73, 93

Kiely, B., 9–16, 32, 34, *35–36*
Kligler-Vilenchik, N., 42
Korman, B., 53
KQED Do Now, 45
Kress, G., 2

Leander, K., 80, 84
Letters to the Next President, 49
Lewison, M., 92–93
literacy, 1–2, 79–81
literary: development, 56–57; instruction, 79–81; lenses theory, 30; media, 87; response, 91;
literature, 22–24, 64
literature circles, 43, 67, 108
The Lizzie Bennet Diaries, 87
Los Angeles Times, 94

mapping tools, 80
marketing, 70
Martin, Kymberly, 106
media: discussions on, 30; literary media and, 87; participatory engagement and, 48; remixes and, 95–96; with teachers, 54, 81; teaching, learning and, 103; YAL and, 81, 115–16. *See also* social media
Melville, Herman, 92
Minecraft, 58

Minecraft Mods, 53
mini-book talks, 66
mobilization, 42, 49
Moby Dick (Melville), 92
Monster (Myers), 44–45
multimedia assessments, 57–60
multimedia projects, 80, 112–13
multimodal: affordances, 14–15; composition, 104–105; dialogue, 84–85; digital, 9; remixes, 93, 95, 99; texts, 1–2, 3, 80
Myers, Walter Dean, 44–45

narratives, 29–31, 91, 103
National Council for Teachers of English (NCTE), 66
National Education Policy Center (NEPC), 63
Navajos, 82–83
Newsweek, 112
next-generation learning, 28
novels, 68, 87; friendship in, 23; procession of voices and, 84–85; teachers on, 83; of YA, 5, 88

"Offline," *111*
Orenstein, Peggy, 112

paradigm shift, 4, 28
participation, 10, 11, 42–43, 48–49, 105
participatory engagement, 48
pedagogical approach, 64–65, 84
pedagogical considerations, 3–5
personalized learning, 22–24
Peterson, P. J., 68
Pew Research Center, 41
photo avatar, 13
photo poem, *102*
Piotrowski, A., 20
Pitts-Wiley, R., 80
Pradl, G., 84
prediscourse activity, 32
preservice teachers, 19–24
Preskill, S., 32
procession of voices, 84–85

producers, 3, 5, 54–55, 105, 115
production, 42, 47–48

reader response, 84–85
readers: on critical literacy, 105–106; critical readers and, 28, 31–32, 43; on digital reading, 16; within Glose, 11–15
reading: critical, 28; as digital devices, 10; events for, 67; historical fiction and, 81; multimodal digital and, 9; students on, 97; teachers on, 54–55, 69; of YAL, 69–70, 74, 116
reconnect phase, 111–12
Red Cedar Writing Project, Michigan State, 44, 46
Reilly, E., 80
reimagination text, 55
relevant literature, 19–20, 28–29
remixes: book trailer and, 98; with critical literacy, 105–6; media and, 95–96; multimodal, 95, 99; students on, 95–96, 99; teachers on, 106; as telling stories, 101
remix products, 95, *96*, 96–98
rewriting, 15–16
Reynolds, J., 9–16, 32, 34, *35–36*
Rob&Sara.com (Peterson and Ruckman), 68
Ruckman, Ivy, 68

Saint Iggy (Going), 92–94, 96–98
Sams, A., 20–21
Sangita, L., 42
Seedfolks (Fleischman), 46–47
Selfe, C. L., 3–4
set-building, 58
Shadow and Bone (Bardugo), 22
Sims, 53, 58
Skype, 73
smartphones, 10–11, 54
Snapchat, 53
social codes, 105
social life, 41–42

social media, 80, 84, *107*; apps and, 72; gaming and, 53–61; *The Great Gatsby* and, 60; multimodal composition and, 104–5; outlets for, 72; posting to, 58; students on, 59, 103, 111
social semiotics, 85–88
Socratic Circles: with digital discussion board, 34; discussions in, 31, 34; goals of, 29; protocol of, 29; questions for, *35–36*; students on, 33; YAL and, 34
Socratic learning, 27–35
Socratic seminars, 70, 85, *86*
Song of Myself (Whitman), 101, 107–109, *109*, *110*
source material, *83*, 95
status update, *59*
Stornaiuolo, A., 80
Storybird, 66, *67*
StoryCorps, 46
student-centered assessments, 57–60
students: on annotation, 14; on anticipation guide, 23; on authentic engagement, 35; on blogging, 69; on book club, 108; on *The Book Thief*, 29; on book trailers, 12; on buzzing, 32–33; on chat box, 68; on classes, 16; in classrooms, 1–6; on collaboration, 56, 60–61, 69, 71–72; on critical dialogues, 45; on critical inquiry, 5; critical lenses and, 91; as critical readers, 43; on culture, 5; on digital citizen, 45; on digital devices, 9–10; on digital discussion board, 33; on digital environments, 4; on digital samples, 113; digital self-portrait contract of, *113–14*; on digital work, 3; on discussions, 108; on education, 97; empowerment of, 3; on final projects, 114–15; final remix products from, *96*; graduate, 92; on inner circle, 31; on Instagram,

115; interactive record of, 33; on Jay Gatsby mansion, *59*; on journal responses, 93; on literary development, 56–57, 91; on literature, 22; on marketing, 70; on microphones, 68; on multimodal remixes, 95, 99; on online discussions, 108; on photo avatar, 13; on policy restrictions, 56; on prediscourse activity, 32; as producers, 54–55; on reading, 97; reflections by, 99; on remixes, 95–96, 99; revisions from, 114; on rewriting, 16; on smartphones, 10–11, 54; on social issues, 104; on social media, 59, 103, 111; on Socratic Circles, 33; teachers on, 15–16; on technology, 71; on texts, 14, 47, 93; on verbal conversations, 32; on videos, 15, 22; on Whitman, 109; on YAL, 47, 71; on YA novel, 71; on Zoom, 70. *See also* virtual students
suicide prevention, 47–49, *48*
summative assessment, 15, 57

teachers: on book activities, 82–83; on civic engagement, 46; on classroom pedagogy, 28–29; on context, 106–108; on critical literacy, 73; on digital tools, 105; on digital work, 5–6; on discussions, 29; on ed tech, 3; on Glose, 11–12, 15–16; on literary media, 87; on media, 54, 81; on multimedia projects, 85, 112–13; on multimodal practices, 80; on novels, 83; on participation, 49; on producers, 55; on projects, 106–108; on reading, 54–55, 69; on remixes, 106; on student engagement, 15–16; on technology, 23; on YAL, 87; on youth, 84. *See also* preservice teachers; virtual teachers

teaching: of digital composition, 104–105; of *The Great Gatsby*, 55–56; media and, 103; with YAL, 64–65
technology: in critical literacy, 105; multimodal texts and, 1–2; on paradigm shift, 4; Socratic learning and, 27–35; students on, 71; teachers on, 23
Teen Book Finder, 73
texts: on critical literacy, 94; reimagination, 55; students on, 14, 47, 93; visual, 2; YA on, 15–16
They Said She Was Crazy (Brickey), 47–48
Thomas, E. E., 80
Trivia Crack, 56
Turner, K. H., 48
Twitter, 72
Tyrell (Booth), 92–94, 97

Van Doren, C., 81–82
Van Sluys, K., 92–93
Vega, Denise, 69
verbal conversations, 32
videos, 15, 20–23, *86*
virtual classrooms, 64–67
virtual education, 63, 65, 73–74
virtual students, 65–66, 69
virtual teachers, 63–66, 72
visual rhetoric, 112

Whitman, Walt: *Song of Myself* by, 101, 107–109, *109–10*; students on, 109; YAL on, 110
Wiggins, G., 81–82
Witte, S., 20

YA. *See* Young Adult
YAL. *See* Young Adult Literature
YALSA. *See* Young Adult Library Services Association
Young Adult (YA), 4, 71; historical fiction and, 81–82, *83*; novels of,

5, 88; on texts, 15–16; titles for, 9, 79
Young Adult Library Services Association (YALSA), 66, 73
Young Adult Literature (YAL), 101–102; civic engagement through, 41–52; critical readers of, 31–32; curriculum and, 64; descriptions of, 106, *107*; digital capabilities of, 74; on digital media, 4; discussions on, 73; ELA and, 41; through engagement, 41–52, 64; flipped learning and, 19–24; investigation and, 46–47; in literature circles, 108; media and, 81, 115–16; mess around with, 87; misunderstanding and, 103; narrative on, 49; novel for, 68, 87; producers of, 5; production and, 47–48; reader response and, 84–85; reading of, 69–70, 74, 116; on relevance, 42; through social issues, 27; social semiotics, 85–88; Socratic Circles and, 34; Socratic seminar of, 85; students on, 47, 71; studying of, 44; teachers on, 87; teaching with, 64–65; in virtual classrooms, 64–67; on Whitman, 110; youth with, 88
youth: Boyd on, 103–104; on critical literacy, 105; literacy practices of, 79; *Saint Iggy* on, 94; teachers on, 84; with YAL, 88
youth literacies, 53–61
youth motifs, 53–61

Zimmerman, A. M., 42
Zoom, 70
Zusak, Markus, 28–29

About the Editors

Steven T. Bickmore is associate professor of English education in the Department of Teaching and Learning in the College of Education at the University of Nevada, Las Vegas (UNLV). He taught high school English in the Jordan School District in the Salt Lake City area from 1980 to 2008. In addition to teaching English courses, including Advanced Placement courses, he taught Latin and humanities. His many teacher awards and recognitions included an NEH/Reader's Digest Teacher Scholar Award (a full-year paid research sabbatical) for the 1989–1990 school year, and he was a winner of the prestigious Milken Educator Award in 1999. He is a cofounder and coeditor of *Study and Scrutiny: Research in Young Adult Literature*. Bickmore began his university teaching at Louisiana State University in 2008 before moving to UNLV in 2015. He has authored or coauthored over thirty academic papers and book chapters and published in a variety of journals.

Jennifer S. Dail is associate professor of English education in the Department of English at Kennesaw State University in Kennesaw, Georgia. She also directs the Kennesaw Mountain Writing Project (KMWP), a National Writing Project (NWP) site serving teachers Pre-K through college in all content areas. She has received multiple grant awards supporting the work of KMWP, including an Improving Teacher Quality grant. Prior to joining the faculty at Kennesaw State University in 2006, she taught English education courses at the University of Alabama and taught middle and high school English. Dail served as coeditor of *SIGNAL Journal*, International Reading Association's journal focusing on young adult literature, from 2008 to 2013. She is also an active member of several educational organizations, including the National Council of Teachers of English (NCTE) and the NWP. She serves on the board for the Georgia Council of Teachers of English (GCTE) as the interim conference director and college liaison. Dail has published multiple articles on young adult literature and technology in the *ALAN Review* and has several book chapters focusing on this work as well.

Shelbie Witte is the Kim and Chuck Watson Chair in Education and associate professor of adolescent literacy and English education at Oklahoma State University, where she directs the Oklahoma State University Writing Project and leads the Initiative for 21st Century Literacies Research. Her research focuses on the intersection of twenty-first-century literacies and pedagogy, particularly at the middle level. She is coeditor, along with Sara Kajder, of NCTE's *Voices from the Middle*.

About the Contributors

Fawn Canady, PhD, is visiting assistant professor at the University of Nevada, Las Vegas, where she has been an adjunct since 2008. Her research interests include visual culture and multimodal composition. An active member of the Southern Nevada Writing Project, she engages in writing, youth, and community.

Matt Copeland is an author, presenter, and instructional coach who works with educators to build capacity in using Socratic Circles in K–12 classrooms and beyond. A former English teacher and department head, he has been recognized as the 2006 Distinguished Kansan of the Year in Education, a 2005 Milken National Educator, and a 2003 Kansas Master Teacher. He is a frequent presenter at local, regional, and national conferences, and has published several books, essays, and poems on the teaching of English.

Dallas Cox recently graduated from Morehead State University with a bachelor of arts in English, concentrated in secondary education, and is an instructor of English at Fleming County High School in Flemingsburg, Kentucky.

Brooke Eisenbach is assistant professor of middle and secondary education at Lesley University. She was a middle school English and young adult literature teacher for nine years, and an English I virtual school teacher for two years. She is an active member of the National Council of Teachers of English (NCTE) and American Educational Research Association (AERA), and a state representative for Assembly on Literature for Adolescents (ALAN). She is a member of NCTE's Standing Committee against Censorship. She is a former recipient of the Florida Council of Teachers of English Teacher of the Year and the NCTE Outstanding Middle Level Educator in the English Language Arts awards.

Jennifer Farnham is a teacher for Florida Virtual School, an online K–12 public school, where she teaches film/theater and social media. She was a middle school language arts teacher for three years and a high school English teacher for ten years. She is passionate about incorporating independent reading in the classroom along with innovative technology and social justice.

Paula Greathouse is assistant professor of secondary English education at Tennessee Tech University. She was a secondary English and reading teacher for sixteen years. She is an active member of the NCTE, Literacy Research Association (LRA), AERA, and a state representative for ALAN. She sits on NCTE's Standing Committee against Censorship, LGBT Advisory Committee, and Gender and Equities Committee. She is a former recipient of the Florida Council of Teachers of English High School Teacher of the Year Award and the NCTE Teacher of Excellence Award. She is currently the chair of the NCTE Standing Committee against Censorship.

Alison Heron-Hruby is assistant professor of English education at Morehead State University in Morehead, Kentucky, and a former middle and high school English teacher. Her research focuses on multimodal literacies, reading comprehension, and the teaching of writing. She has published in *Journal of Adolescent and Adult Literacy*, *Reading and Writing Quarterly*, and *English Journal*.

Lindsay Ellis Johnson is an instructor of English III and Advanced Placement Language and Composition at Rowan County Senior High School in Morehead, Kentucky. She is an accomplished mentor of preservice English teachers and a teacher leader/coauthor on a National Writing Project College-Ready Writers grant. She has presented at the Writing Eastern Kentucky Conference, the Kentucky Council of Teachers of English Conference, and the National Council of Teachers of English Conference.

Sara B. Kajder, PhD, is a member of the English Education faculty at the University of Georgia. Her research and pedagogical writing explore questions related to our uptake of digital tools in support of readers and writers, teacher practices with digital tools and social media, and implications for teacher education. She is the author of several practitioner books, including the 2012 James Britton Award winning *Adolescents and Digital Literacies*. Dr. Kajder received the 2016 Divergent Award for Excellence in 21st Century Literacies and the 2017 National Technology Leadership Fellowship in English Education. She currently coedits the NCTE's journal *Voices from the Middle* with Shelbie Witte.

Kymberly Martin is a high school English teacher in Las Vegas, Nevada, and an adjunct professor at the University of Nevada, Las Vegas, in the

Department of Teaching and Learning, Literacy. She teaches honors and AP courses. Kym has worked as a project facilitator for the Clark County School District developing innovative professional development (PD) for new teachers and mentors. She has also designed PD around project-based learning. Kym has worked closely with UNLV researchers to pursue research in meaningful, creative, and identity-affirming curriculum for high school students.

Jenny Cameron Paulsen is an instructional coach at Holmes Junior High School in Cedar Falls, Iowa. A junior high and high school English and history teacher for twenty-three years, she is a past president of the Iowa Council of Teachers of English and an ardent advocate for the Iowa Writing Project. A graduate of Iowa State University and the University of Northern Iowa, she is passionate about spreading hope, conversational learning, genealogy, archery, and knitting. She lives on a farm with her husband and teenage son.

Amy Piotrowski is assistant professor of secondary education and English education at Utah State University Uintah Basin. Before becoming a teacher educator, she was a middle school and high school English teacher.

Dawn Reed is an English teacher at Okemos High School in Okemos, Michigan. Dawn is also codirector of the Red Cedar Writing Project at Michigan State University. Dawn earned her master's degree in writing and rhetoric with a specialization in critical studies in literacy and pedagogy from Michigan State University. She conducts PD for teachers focused on technology integration and the teaching of writing. She is coauthor of *Research Writing Rewired: Lessons That Ground Students' Digital Learning* and *Real Writing: Modernizing the Old School Essay*, and she has published in various journals, books, and websites.

Chyllis E. Scott is assistant professor of literacy at UNLV. She graduated from Texas A&M University with a PhD in curriculum and instruction with an emphasis in literacy education. Prior to earning her doctorate, Dr. Scott was a classroom teacher, English as a Second Language teacher and department head, codirector of Advancement Via Individual Determination (AVID) and gifted and talented education programs, and a school-wide reading specialist. Her primary research interests include adolescent literacy and content-area literacy instruction, teacher education and knowledge, and mentoring practices in higher education.

Robyn Seglem is associate professor of middle-level English language arts and literacy at Illinois State University. Researching on technology's role in literacy, adolescent literacy, and content area literacy, her work has been published in *Teachers College Record*, *Journal of Adolescent and Adult Literacy*, *English Journal*, *Voices from the Middle*, and *Journal of Language and Literacy Education*. She teaches literacy courses to middle and secondary preservice and graduate teachers from twenty content areas. She is a nationally board certified teacher and has taught for nine years in middle and high school language arts.

Anna Smith is assistant professor of secondary education at Illinois State University. She is the coauthor of *Developing Writers: Teaching and Learning in the Digital Age*, and a coeditor of *Handbook of Writing, Literacies, and Education in Digital Cultures*. Her research on writing development, transliteracies, educational technologies, and the intersection of teaching and learning can be found in the *Journal of Literacy Research*, *Education Sciences*, *English Journal*, and *Literacy*. Her scholarly work is buttressed with eighteen years of work in public schools as a teacher, district-level teaching specialist, and teacher educator.

Dakoda Trenary recently graduated from Morehead State University with a Bachelor of Arts in English, concentrated in secondary education, and is an instructor of English at Rowan County Senior High School in Morehead, Kentucky.

Kristen Hawley Turner, PhD, is associate professor of English education and contemporary literacies at Fordham University. Her research focuses on the intersections between technology and literacy, and she works with teachers across content areas to implement effective literacy instruction and incorporate technology in meaningful ways. She is the coauthor of *Connected Reading: Teaching Adolescent Readers in a Digital World* and *Argument in the Real World: Teaching Students to Read and Write Digital Texts*. She is also a teacher consultant for the National Writing Project and director of the Fordham Digital Literacies Collaborative.

Aneté Vásquez is associate professor of curriculum and instruction at Kennesaw State University. She teaches courses in English/language arts and general education in the Department of Secondary and Middle Grade Education. Her research interests include all aspects of the clinical preparation of teachers, particularly in the area of preparing teacher candidates to work with diverse learners.

www.ingramcontent.com/pod-product-compliance
Lightning Source LLC
Chambersburg PA
CBHW020748230426
43665CB00009B/535